TABLE OF CONTENT

Acknowledgements 5
This Charming Man, foreword by Simon Bank 6
About the Authors 8
Introduction 12

1. A theoretical introduction 14

2. How to think statistically 28

3. Rotations 34
   - Introduction 34
   - The most important spaces 38
   - Versus Spain, World cup 2010 40
   - Attacking phases 44
   - Implementation of rotations 46
   - 5v3 50
   - 7v5 56
   - 9v7 60
   - 10v9 64

4. Summary 68

5. Interchanges in the final third 72
   - Introduction and methodology 72
   - 5v1 (Starting Positions) 76
   - Interchange exercises 78

6. Case Manchester United 94
   - Build up 96
   - Principles of play Athletic Bilbao 100
   - Entries 102

7. Summary 104

8. The Platform 106

9. Coach Education 108

10. References 110

ACKNOWLEDGEMENTS

Finally putting pen to paper and creating this book has been a long and winding road for both of us. Occupied by the everyday business of club and national team duties - this has been a source of constant bad conscience.

But now with the ink dry, we would like to express our heartfelt gratitude to Mats Heed, FM Reklam - our sponsor for this endeavor. Thanks for your patience - your support and your constant positive spirit put us in a position that we could pull this one off.

Brian Clarhaut - without your research and constant eye on the horizon we wouldn't have the insights and inspiration for this book. You are one of the main reasons that this book ever got to see the light of the day.

All the coaching courses, instructors, fellow coaches and friends that really questioned us and stimulated constant discussions about football. And all the people that really want to improve the football world, both from top down and bottom up.

Our families - the late hours & the long discussions that took away some obvious family hours are by far the greatest dedication and token of love you ever could've given us.

Last - and not least. All the players that've been unwitting guinea pigs for all the testing and weird stuff they've been doing on the pitch – thank you! We realize we have also been wasting a lot of your time – we're grateful to say the least!

Copyright © 2019 by Hans Backe and John Wall

All rights reserved. No part of this publication may be reproduced, distributed, or transmitted in any form or by any means, including photocopying, recording, or other electronic or mechanical methods, without the prior written permission of the publisher, except in the case of brief quotations embodied in critical reviews and certain other noncommercial uses permitted by copyright law. For permission requests, write to the publisher, addressed "Attention: Permissions Coordinator," at the address below.

Backe Konsult AB
Olovsvägen 9
Sundbyberg, 172 76
www.rotaciones.com

THIS CHARMING MAN

So they call him El Loco. The Madman.
They take a look at him, pacing, walking from line to line in the technical area, count the number of turns (13) he's making until he sits down, stands up, starts again. Pattern in the madness. And then there are all the anecdotes, the stories, the conflicts that add depth to the narrative. How he faced violent Rosario Central Italicize Barras Bravas with a hand grenade in his hand. The 50 000 matches he's studied in order to find the 28 possible modules to break down an organized defense. The towers he built to watch training sessions from above, the tussle with a construction worker in Bilbao who didn't satisfy his standards. The way he left Marseille, Lille, the way he let Lazio down after two days in charge. All those stories.

Over the years, all sorts of football dignitaries have tried to find a method in the madness that is Marcelo Bielsa, only to find that they got the fundamental question wrong. Thing is, with Bielsa you have to start with the notion that it's the other way around: madness in the method. In the modern game, managers and coaches all talk about attention to detail as an absolute necessity, but only a few of them have (pun not totally unintended) walked the walk.

To Bielsa, attention to detail means studying those 50 000 videotapes, getting to know every player in the youth set-up by first name, taking Sanchez, Isla and Vidal out to the training pitch for hours on end, or spending day and night doing video analysis with his assistants. To Bielsa, being serious means living in a six square meter room in Santiago for a few years to be fully, truly, madly, deeply devoted to the cause. I've been fascinated by Marcelo Bielsa since the first time I stepped into that vast footballing universe of his, and it's even fair to say that he, on multiple occasions, saved my love for the sport. When so much in the modern game made me disillusioned, he made me curious. When a whole lot seemed stupid and negative, he stood out with his brilliant mind and positive, attacking, idealistic football.

Like his siblings, he could have been a lawyer or a politician, an architect or a minister of foreign affairs. Instead he chose football, stepped right into the dialectic void left by Menotti and Bilardo and walked his very own way. There are two sides to Bielsa's football, and I love both. Firstly, there's the intellectual honesty, the ambition. He sees football as a science and acts accordingly, and I trust this book to dig deep into that science. Secondly, and more importantly: There's the raw passion.

For all the interesting groundwork, if his teams hadn't performed, no one would care. But they did. Not all the time, and certainly not for a very long time. But they did. Back in 2012, I walked through a sun-kissed Bilbao to watch Bielsa's Athletic hold a master class with Alex Ferguson's Manchester United being the students. The old, shabby San Mamés stadium, was literally bouncing as Athletic ran riot on the pitch, following the main principles of his football to the letter. They pressured, high and hard. They outnumbered United at the back. The ran, ran, and ran some more. They won 2–1, they could easily have hit United for six. It was, by all standards, good football. From an intellectual standpoint, but first and foremost from an emotional perspective: It was passionate, it was idealistic, it was a brand of football which could lead a people through the desert. As we sat down for the post-match presser, with Marcelo Bielsa staring at the desk in front of him, someone asked the manager what he made of the atmosphere. You could hear the supporter party cascading down the streets outside the stadium.
– "Well", said Bielsa, "I'm not totally unmoved by it."
Marcelo Bielsa knows everything, but more than anything he makes people believe. He may lack certain people skills and that little bit of pragmatism that some of his disciples – Simeone, Sampaoli, Pochettino, even Guardiola to some extent – have added, but he has been one of few who has been abled to change not only the way football is played, but the way we understand the sport. That is his greatest gift to the game.
Mad as it may be.   /By Simon Bank

ABOUT THE AUTHORS

Hans Backe
I am currently working as a pundit for TV4 and CMore in Sweden. I started work as a coach/manager since 1979. I am fortunate enough to have worked as a coach for AIK, Djurgårdens IF, Hammarby and Östers IF in Sweden, in Norway with Molde and Stabaek., in Denmark with Aalborg and FC Copenhagen, in Austria for Salzburg, and in Greece for Panathinaikos.

As an assistant manager I worked for Sven-Göran Eriksson in Manchester City and the Mexican Men's National Team and as a Manager for Notts County. My most recent club job was for the New York Red Bulls in Major League Soccer. My most recent role was a head coach for the Finnish national team.

My first encounter with Marcelo Bielsa was during a friendly game against Chile with Mexico back in 2008. I was completely baffled by the movement and work capacity of the Chilean players. Feeling almost powerless at the sidelines, I've been a follower and admirer of Bielsa ever since.

This book has been almost five years in the making, but it's been worth it on so many ways.

And yes, I do love the Smiths.

John Wall
Currently working as a CEO for Game Insight Soccer, a company which educates coaches and players in game insight. A company that strives to create a deeper understanding of the game, and in the end - give access to what the players do and how they solve situations on the field.

I've been working as a coach for the past 15 years on different levels, including a spell together with Hans in the Men's National Team of Finland.

I've always been drawn to the outlier, the underdog or someone who does it differently and reaches that height of things that I didn't quite think were possible, or even at times didn't even know existed. Marcelo Bielsa is one, if not THE ONE that I've admired for such a long time. This book represents just a small fragment of his monumental philosophy and vision of the game.

John is UEFA A-license and A-License Youth Elite holder.

And yes, I do love the Smiths.

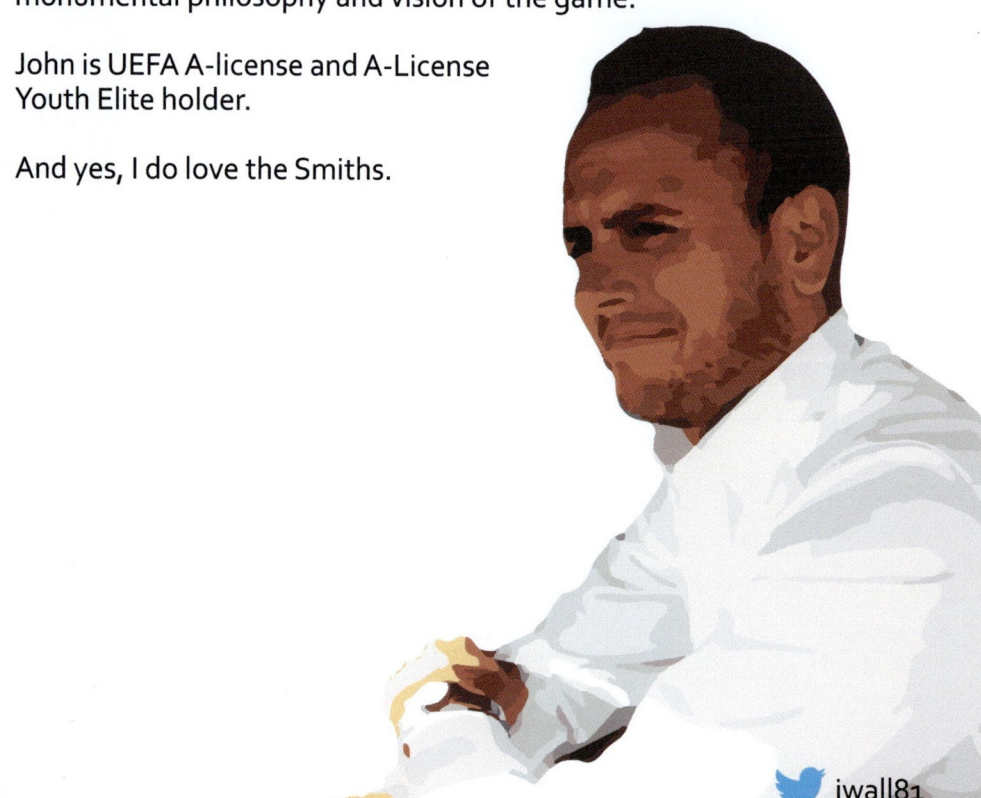

jwall81

"*Out in the blue and into the black – they give you this but you pay for that And once you're gone, you can never come back When you're out of the blue and into the black*"

Extract from My My, Hey Hey by Neil Young

INTRODUCTION

The constant quest for winning can result in some periods of getting the upper hand for a short while, cause eventually people will catch up. Our aim with this book is to inspire, to a realistic extent, the objective facts within football - as well as your playing philosophy. If you want to act as a copy cat and take the x's and o's straight into you situation - you are more or less likely to fail. What fits you and your situation (objective facts coupled with external factors) is precisely the thought process we want to stimulate you as a reader into. We deliberately want to put you into problems, funny right? And to quote from Cemetery Gates by The Smiths:

But I've read well, and I've heard them said
A hundred times (maybe less, maybe more)
If you must write prose/poems
The words you use should be your own
Don't plagiarize or take "on loan"
Cause there's always someone, somewhere
With a big nose, who knows
And who trips you up and laughs
When you fall
Who'll trip you up and laugh
When you fall

If you literally didn't catch our subtle way of not making a clear copy paste of our work. And it all starts with yourself - cause your players are all originals, not Tabula Rasa. So start by acting on your own, start treating your player as capable of such as well. They are all the future stars, unique in their own way. Inspired yes - clones no.

By this book - we want to express our inspiration of the great Marcelo Bielsa. Perhaps not the most title winning coach - but perhaps the most innovative coach of our time. More so, the coaches he's directly influenced are beyond astonishing. Guardiola, Pochettino, Sampaoli form a short list of coaches that've been openly appreciative by his mentoring and inspiration. And our own description of Bielsa football - Football on crack.

It's easy to consume Football - wins, losses and draws. But putting that aside, what actually really rocks you and shakes your beliefs? Historically there's been a few games that changed Football - Hungary's mauling of England 1953 (The Flying Magyars) is still seen as one of those games. For us in many ways, it's the two games between Athletic Bilbao and Manchester United in the 2012 Europa League. Monumentally, the way Bilbao's players outran and outmaneuvered United changed our view upon how the game can be played. How much can you demand of your players in a game? Can you create desired "set situations" in open play? How can you manipulate the opposition just as it seemed that the Bilbao's players were doing with United's players?

And in order to channel on how much we could go into within one book, we felt that mainly our focus should be:

Rotations - in build up to create space and create positive entries through the opponent.

Interchanges - changing positions when it comes to create goalscoring chances and create positive entries into the penalty box.

Thus, this book will be presented in a theoretical way and by giving examples through QR-codes shared in every chapter and certain sections to give even more life to our theoretical framework. We want to enhance our product and give more of an experience to you - there's always more to learn!

For a more liberated football - ENJOY!

01 A THEORETICAL INTRODUCTION

What is Football?

A game can be distinguished with four characteristics. Each game is characterized by (1) a goal (2) means for achieving that goal (3) rules and (4) the voluntary acceptance of these rules. These characteristics are inseparably linked together[1]. We can therefore conclude that Football is a game, whereas the objective is to win, by scoring one goal more than the opponent. But what follows is the objective means that we're all slaves to.

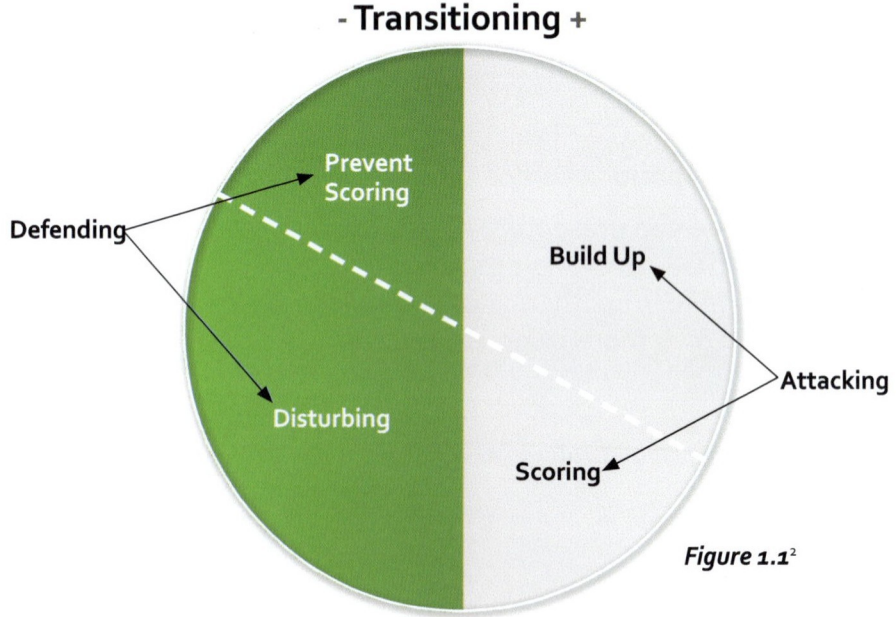

Figure 1.1[2]

---

[1] Tamboer, Jan W.I. Football Theory, p. 24 World Football Academy
[2] Tamboer, Jan W.I. Football Theory, p. 61 World Football Academy

By far, football is the sport where you have to perform the greatest amount of actions in order to get even remotely close to what it all comes down to.

We can conclude that a team's functions are governed by Attacking - Transition - Defending. Therefore the team's tasks are situated around these phases. If you are attacking therefore, the tasks could be Build Up - Passing - Creating Space (Forwards - Backwards - Sideways). But the fact is there is this opponent whose sole purpose is to make life harder for you.

How to outline the steps/parts in football
11v11 is the amount of players that's playing on a regular full size field in football. The complexity of the game, and in a way it's simplicity is an effect of the size of the field, amount of players and the functions and task of the team. And the individual is bound by those constraints within the universal time and space question. We will hereby conclude on how to view on how you can seek to understand the game and it inherent limitations. We conclude that the model presented by Tamboer in Football Theory gives a unique summary of Football and it's objective parts (Attachment 1)

But in what order does it all come together?
The game is a predefinition on **what** is going on during a game and **why** it looks as it looks. Although - the How is a whole different thing. You have the ball. You have 10 teammates. You have 11 opponents against you. The biggest understatement is would be that "you probably would have to collaborate in order to score a goal."

The framework we would suggest in this would be:
Understand the Game.
Find ways of how to collaborate
Understand Objective Principles
Then seek to organize your team - define Roles/Positions
Apply your subjective principles in harmony with the Game-Collaboration- Objective Principles - Your organization/Positions/Roles
And remember you're never finished in that perspective. There is always processes and most importantly - it never becomes real until you fully understand your players and that they can contribute in their own way.

"*There is a Light that never Goes Out*"

Objective Attacking Principles
For every action - there will be a reaction. We will outline, in this book, a primary focus on **Attacking** - How to create space away from an opponent or create space for a teammate. We want to be more specific in this perspective, and will try to avoid stepping into trying to explain the whole game and still being specific simultaneously. Therefore we will only introduce a few objective principles:

Ballcarrier becoming a teammate
You have the ball as a team, thus attacking. We have established common ground on that passing is probably a good way to collaborate when trying to achieve the highest aim of the game - scoring.
Once the ball carrier has passed the ball to a teammate, the roles change. And what is the task of the teammate?
1) Create new passing options (Forward - Sideways - Backwards)
2) Create time/ space for the ballcarrier
3) Find space whereas you can create a goalscoring chance for the team

Furthermore, we would like the roles to be viewed upon as equal and complementary. If the player on the ball is solely responsible with finding solutions on how to play the ball to a teammate in a favorable situation then it might be the case that your passing in your team might not be as effective as it should be.

> **Further thought**
> What would be the objective defensive principle to deal with a role switch?
> In what way would you present it to your players prior to a session?
> How would you coach it during a session?
> Repetition is the mother of knowledge as they say - how do you make sure that these principles are always incorporated in your sessions?

Playing the ball forward

To play the ball forward and bypass the opponent is the best pass, but the factual reality (time-space-opponent) doesn't always invite this. Therefore we should have the framework of passing hierarchy:

1) Forward pass which while bypassing the opponents is leading to a goal opportunity
2) Forward pass
3) Diagonal pass
4) Sideways pass
5) Backwards pass

> *"The opponent will always give away what you should do"*
>
> /Juanma Lilo

The definition of the most important space

With the aim of the game being to score one more goal than the opponent - we can conclude as follows:
- Where do I increase the probability of scoring?
- Where is the 2nd most interesting space after that?
- Where is the 3rd most interesting space after that?
- And the 4th most interesting space would be?

Deduction:

Golden Zone - space usually behind the opposition center backs is the most attractive space to score a goal.

The space behind the fullbacks is the 2nd most interesting space since it is behind the fullbacks and nearer the penalty box.

The space between the defenders is the 3rd most attractive space (shot from distance, or providing a final pass opportunity)

And as the 4th most interesting space is in front of the backline (shot from distance, final pass - pass out to a cross attempt).

01
HOW CAN I STIMULATE AND IMPROVE THIS PROCESS?

How can you stimulate and become actually good in the corresponding training process

Steal without conscience in the beginning. What do you see? After you get your experience with someone else's adaption of objective and unique external factors - you start to realize you want to do something that's actually yours.

And if you want to be exceptional at something - you need to actually put in some serious dedicated time.

But let's start with simple things. Basics will never go out of style - black is always in. Never underestimate the power of repetition. Be humble enough to realize that you always need to perfect your skills. Create a daily routine where you focus just 5 min on something that you want to become better at - self-reflection.

Remember what you actually did today - do it better tomorrow. Don't make excuses when things are not working out - take responsibility.

Didactics

What difference does it make?

Progression is essential in football. But also the start, and the end. But the end is never the end, but merely the beginning of another end.

An exercise is merely a shell, limited by its outer constraints. Whereas you give a lesser degree of freedom in the beginning, you'll need to expand the degrees of freedom in order to make it all more realistic.

Didactics is merely the theoretical framework and methodological starting points – especially when it comes balancing of theory and practice.

Didactics is the concept which origin is the Greek word didáskein which means to teach, analyze and educate. Didactics refers to the theory and practice of teaching and the learning. It also refers to theoretical departure points and models which can be used to analyze and understand teaching and how the actual teaching should takes place. Didactics can give knowledge on how to look at where teaching and learning is taking place.[2]

The didactical questions

The classical question within didactics: what, how and why? To the "what" question belongs to what we should teach, thus the content and the aim of the teaching. The "why"-question refers to why we should choose that certain content and not something else. It also refers to on how the players can be motivated to learn that specific content.

How" takes its starting point based on the reflection on the previous questions (what-why) and how the teaching should be conducted. To add things up, certain more didactic questions has been discussed over the course of history, not least the **who**-question. Who should be in charge off the actual content of the education?[3]

That is probably a question that's been discussed over the years in football clubs too, especially when it comes to youth players. Would you like to work in a club where everyone acts on their own with their teams? To what extent can the club allow a certain amount of freedom for their coaches to act within their curriculum (player development plan).

A recommendation is that coaches are well educated to apply developmental-and behavior psychological theory while teaching their subjects. But common ground on WHY and WHAT should be accepted and agreed upon at a very minimum. Taking everything into context - and eventually adapting it to your style is key. Style is always a choice - context isn't. But the noise always starts with a different starting point (social media, media).

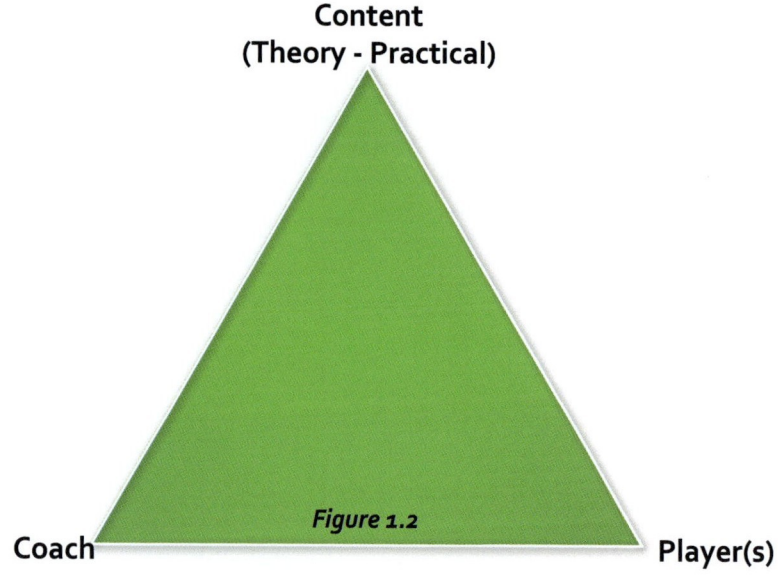

Figure 1.2

Nonetheless, the what of football is always to score one more goal than the opponent, thus winning the game. But setting yourself apart from others is actually to have a clear sense of your "why". If you start communicating why you're doing things in a certain manner, and that they are aligned with the "what" with football - your mix can actually be something worthwhile - and a stronger sense of purpose for you and your players.

In the following diagram we will give a further elaborate a visualization on how we see and adapt context (simplification of a problem, which originates from the actual game, 11v11).

[2,3] www.skolverket.se "Didaktik - vad, hur och varför" 2018-05-09 11.35

OVERVIEW OF A

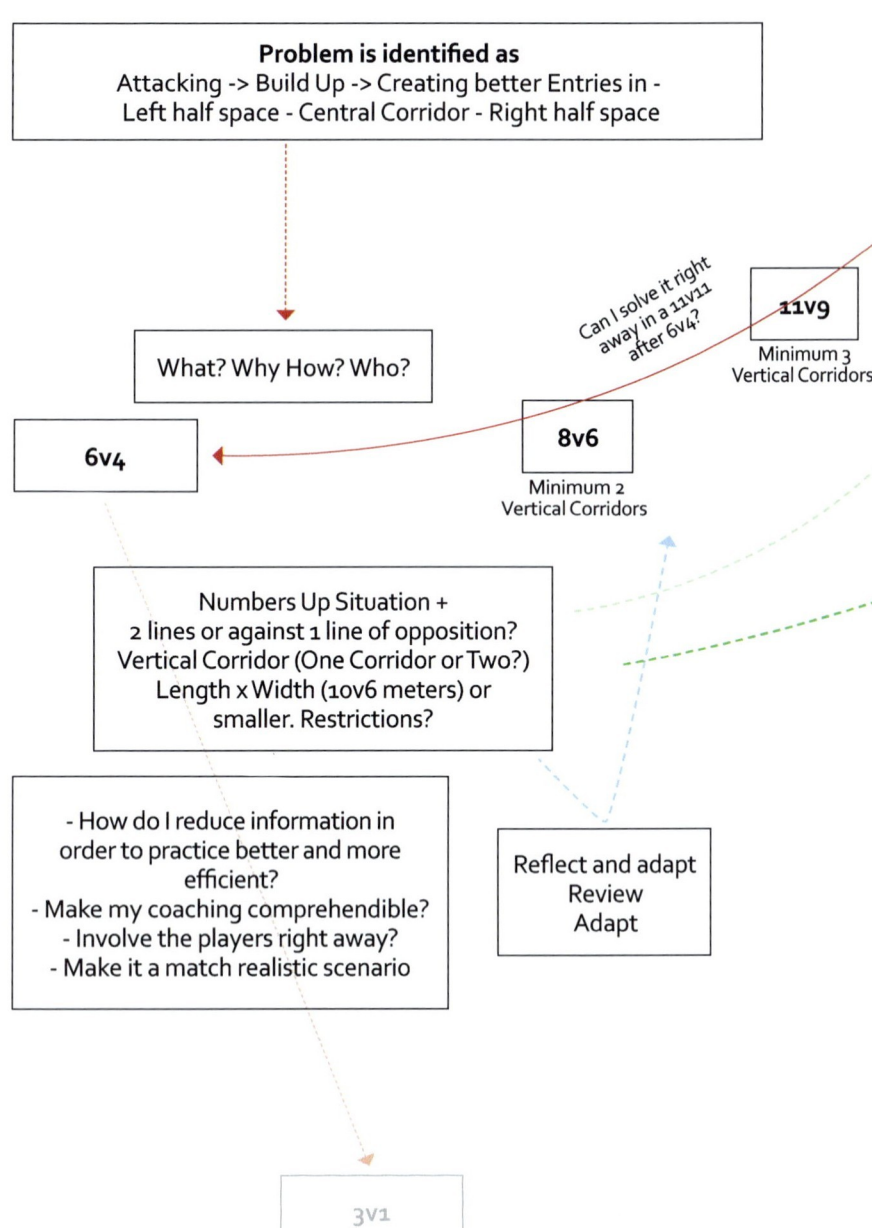

Numbers Up situation +

THINKING PROCESS

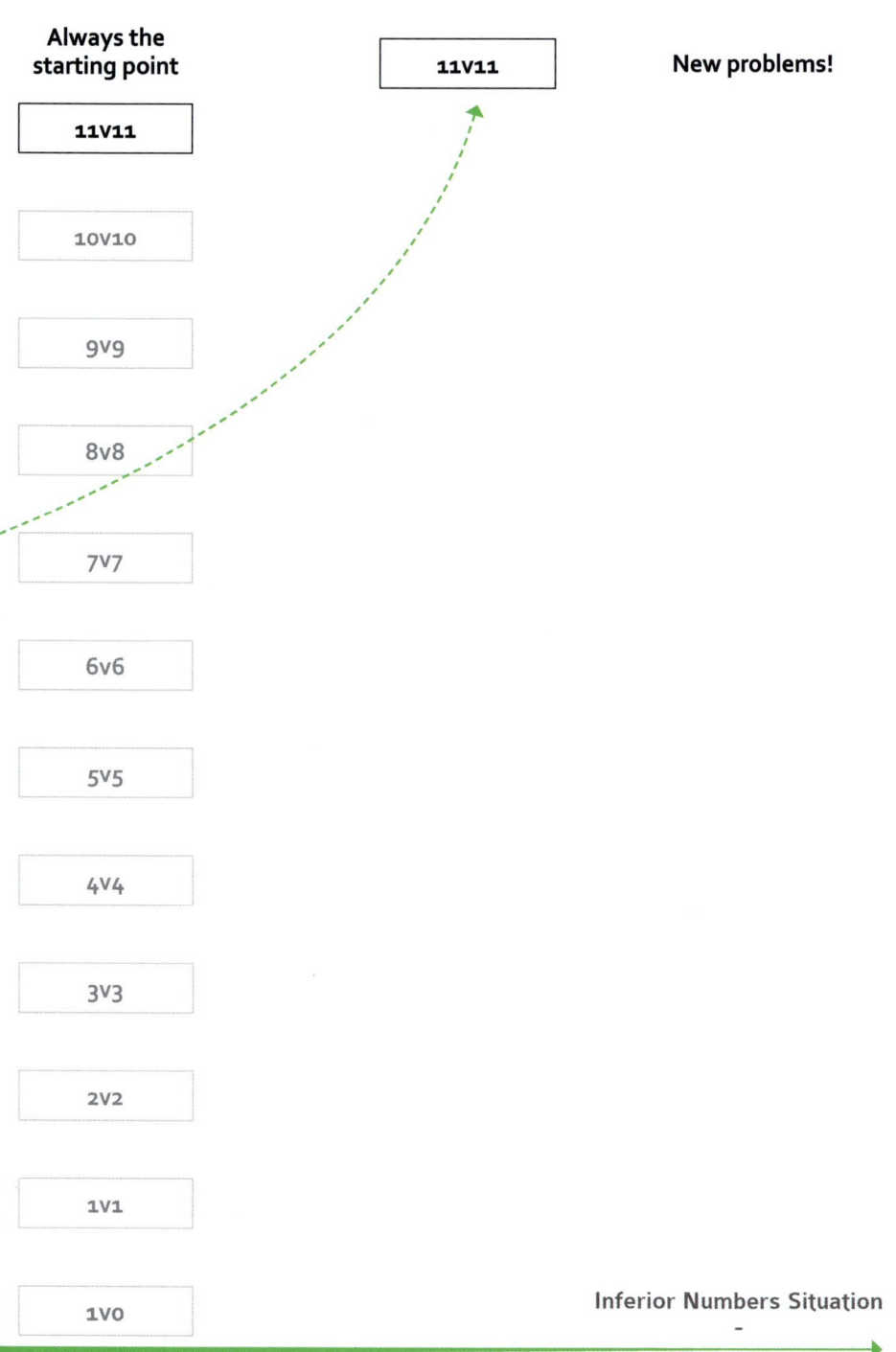

Figure 1.3

"THE BOY WITH A THORN IN HIS SIDE"

How to deal with the full game
Hopefully there has been progression, you've challenged yourself and your players enough to take the game to new levels. And as it should be, it's more down to you and how your players deal with problems.

"When dealing with the full game, things might get overwhelming - but only if you allow it to be. And if it is overwhelming for you - imagine how your players feel it is the case for you"

So without creating too much confirmation bias into what you're looking for, try to have a certain distance while they're playing. Try to keep an objective approach to events - can I provide a proper guidance or aid the players decision making out there?

Try to everyday remember the following:
- How much time do I spend on what to do, and how to do it?
- Focus on your delivery
- Don't let yourself get in the way of the players experience and development
- Never expect that everything's great, enjoy that there's always problems that needs to be taken care of
- Don't fix anything - it has to be a joint operation between the coach and the player. If not so, things will never be fixed or improved. Steel only becomes steel once it meets fire, right?
- Review yourself after each session, don't beat yourself up - but ask more of yourself - good habits trickle down in the organization (players). It all starts with YOU!
- How much are you willing to embody the bigger idea than yourself (the Game Model - Values) - day in and day out
- Be ready to reflect, reframe, refocus (re-re-re). The only thing you can do is RE-ally do it better than the what the work you previously did.

"Lack of clarity and demands lead to a lack of understanding which leads to a lack of agreement, and a lack of agreement spells dishonesty and disaster"
//Bertrand Russell

You can all copy your way forward - but it will only lead you to a certain level, which is not particularly high and it probably doesn't match your ambitions either. Evidently you can't make bricks without clay, to paraphrase Sherlock Holmes. Even more so, the actual clay in the full game might be the thing happening prior to the actual problem. Evidently, football is more of a chain of events than just isolated bricks. Think about this example:

Problem:
You have a problem in your Defending - you keep letting certain type of goals in.

Possible solution:
Look into your Attacking - Do you constantly give your ball away?
Is it when you're trying to make an entry to the final third?

So - when looking at this chain - work yourself fbackwards first, in order to create a better chain with a better outcome.

01

PICTURE AND OVERVIEW OF A WAY

Defending ←   **- Transi**

Effect
We continuously have problems with allowing goalscoring chances. Especially we have a tendency to be numerical disadvantage.

Details+++
What is more frequent than one off?
Look for flaws

Details++
Our reaction to when we evidently have lost the ball? What's the reaction from the player furthest away from the ball?

Prevent Scoring

Disturbing

OF THINKING (CAUSE AND EFFECT)

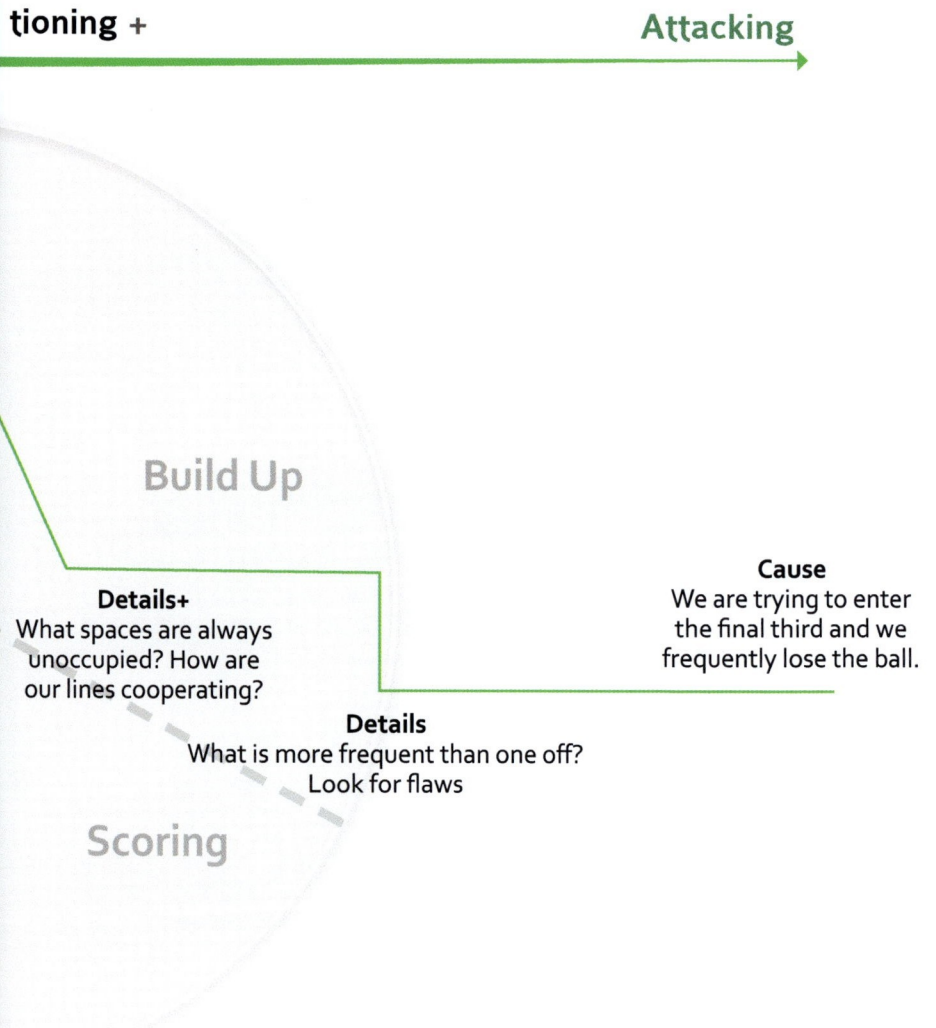

Figure 1.4

HOW SHOULD I THINK WHEN CONSTRUCTING EXERCISES?

Stop Me If You Think You've Heard This One Before

> *Nothing's changed, I still love you, oh, I still love you Only slightly, only slightly less than I used to, my love*

Every exercise should be a simplification of 11v11, therefore designing and implementing the exercise in as much of a game-like state as possible is desirable.

- Where can we make sure to find situations that are frequently occurring during a game?
- Are there certain "things that should be" that you wish your team should distinctly be better at (in order to achieve to first priority - scoring one more goal than the opponent).
- Is there certain traits of your team that you should use to your benefit?
- How do I make it competitive?
- How will I progress from my chosen starting point?
- My coaching points?
- What kind of players do I have at my disposal?
- How much information can I give during one session. I got a quick one for you. Less is more
- Is it directional?
- Do I have a clear understanding of the work/rest ratio?
- Will there be sufficient repetitions?
- How can I tweak/argument the exercise so it actually works to its potential
- Are my players the goal or are they simply just the means for some other goal?
- Are the players being faced with problems to solve against opposition?

HOW TO THINK STATISTICALLY

By Ola Lidmark-Eriksson and Joakim Plogell, Playmaker AI

How to think statistically

You have a problem in your Defending - you keep letting certain type of goals in.

Possible solution:
Look into your Attacking - Do you constantly give your ball away? Is when you're trying to make an entry to the final third?

Step 1 - the unbiased data collection contract.
Start with deciding the level of ambition. How much time do I have for analyzing my teams games. Be honest to yourself since it really is important that you can be consistent in what you analyze over time. Let's say you make an agreement to yourself that you can spend 1 hour after every game for data analysis.

Step 2 - what do we want to know?
If winning the ball in opponents half is key for you game - measure that. If Long throw-ins and short corners are a key for creating shots - measure that. A key for most coaches and somewhat a least common denominator would be to at least look into shots taken and conceded together with what created different chances (buildup/attack type).

Step 3 - gather some data!

Using Codeplay we will look at all the chances the opponents created the last game. Actions are tagged with attack type and we get instant feedback of xG and xP as well as cue points for the right place in the game video. Remember your level of ambition but

tagging a game like this is absolutely not more than one hour of work.

Step 4 - analyze!

Using Codeplay like we do in this example generating a report looking at the number of attacks you got against you from a lost ball is a matter of two clicks. But this really isn't the most interesting...

Step 5 - consistency.

... that is when you remember step 1. Given that you have analysed all your teams game you now have the power to answer the questions that matter in data analysis.
In this example i.e. Does our attempts to make

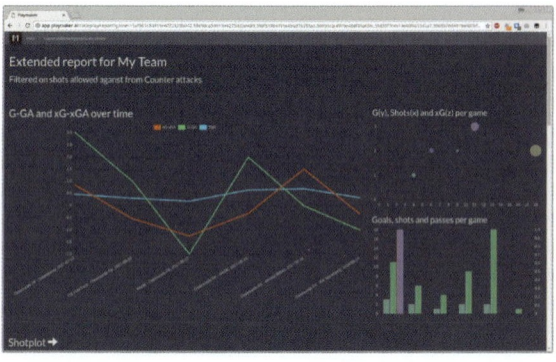

entries into the final third generate more xG for us than against us? What games during the season stood out - positively and negatively? What did we do different then?

> **And remember:**
> Doing more work is not necessarily better. Tagging every action in a game is hardly ever warranted.

So what can thinking more statistically and more logically do for your coaching? Could there always be more than the simple scratch on the surface, and the occasional "bar conclusions" you are building your so called "truth" on?

Now let that sink in for a while. Address your "instant truths" for a while. Have I really understood them - or have I missed the point? Let's try a stoic way of looking at these things:

Coaching Stoicism
(example how to make priorities in your coaching)

Define the problem →	How do I prevent it? →	Repair
In our build up we don't bypass the opponent as frequently is I would like.	Create constraints and manipulate rules/other constraints in games and exercises.	Make It more visible for for the players by visualizing times when they could (bypass the opponent). Give other types of support and coaching.
1.	1.	1.
2.	2.	2.
3.	3.	3.
4.	4.	4.

Figure 2.1

Adaption of Tim Ferriss keynote

https://www.ted.com/talks/tim_ferriss_why_you_should_define_your_fears_instead_of_your_goals

ROTA

TIONS

 ROTATIONS

"Is it really so strange?"

> **Definition of a Rotation**
> The act or process of turning around a center or an axis - a single or complete cycle of such motion.

And we would like to define that a rotation can be done when you're Attacking - Building Up as a team. Rotation in itself and the identification of its beneficiaries is something to unravel and create more understanding about.

Let's start with the end first - if you can score when you have the ball - you should. But that reality is probably something different. And if you look at what kind of actions you do as a team when you're attacking, passing and creating space would probably be pretty-high up on that list.

But - what your opponent would probably do to you prior to your chance to do so is disrupt your build up. And the best pass, no matter what team is playing the game - and with what style - would still be the pass the bypasses the entire opposition - and is tapped in by a player in your team. But that is also probably not the usual case but rather an exceptional one. And Football is, probably by far, the sport in which you have to perform the most amount of actions successfully before the thing that really matters happens and impacts the scoreboard - a goal.

So - how can we play forward as many times as possible in every situation we end up in with the ball? (Attacking)

The following questions is something you should bear in mind:

1) When my goalkeeper has the ball in our build up - what potential problems can he/she have in playing the ball forward?
2) When one of my central defenders has the ball - what potential problems can he/she have in playing the ball forward?
3) When one of my central midfielders has the ball - what potential problems can he/she have in playing the ball forward?
4) When one of my Forwards has the ball - what potential problems can he/she have in playing the ball forward?

Obviously factors such as opponents - available space - where you are on the field - your teammates. But theory is a starting point - what would be your most ideal situation? Try to work yourself from that situation and create the framework. What we will present to you is one of many possible solutions.

Because what kind of problems can the opponent cause you?
They can press you - the can deny space by covering passing lanes and cover for a pressing teammate. They can drop and be very compact in order to deny the most important space of all - the Golden Zone.

> **Clear distinction**
> But - the most clear distinction for us is that you can rotate in your Build Up - you interchange positions/space when it comes to the final pass or entry into the penalty box.

Vertical Rotation

Priority 1, Vertical Rotation: Creating space to bypass the opponent - if not pass to the closest player best positioned for a better entry at the next instance.

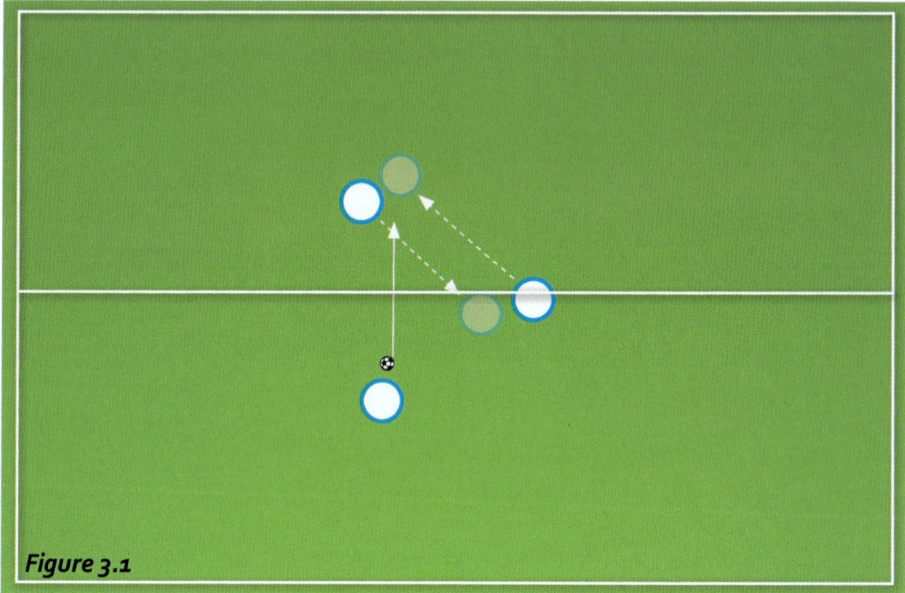

Figure 3.1

Vertical Ex 1

Horizontal Rotation

Priority 2, Horizontal Rotation: Create space above and the space for a different entry near the ballcarrier.

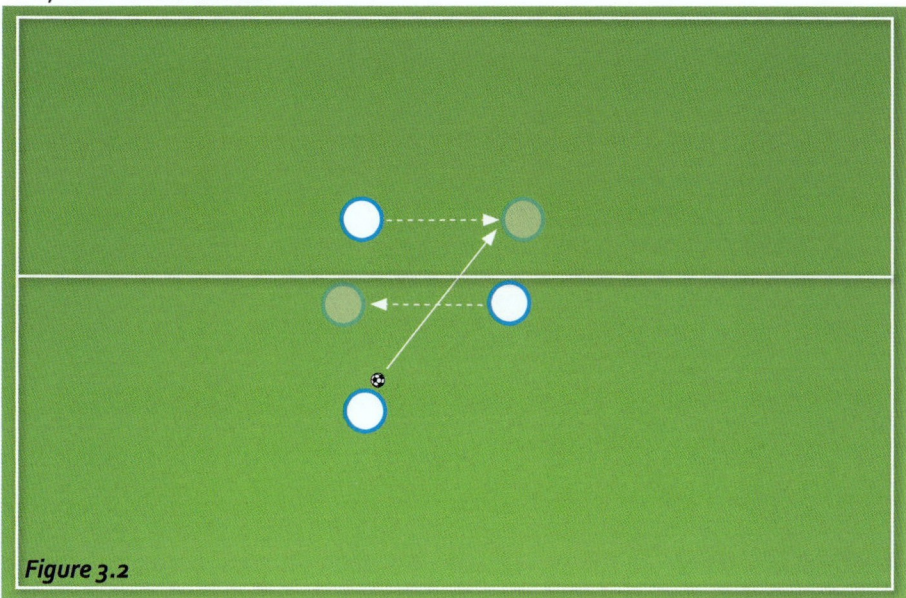

Figure 3.2

Rotation Ex2

THE MOST IMPORTANT SPACES

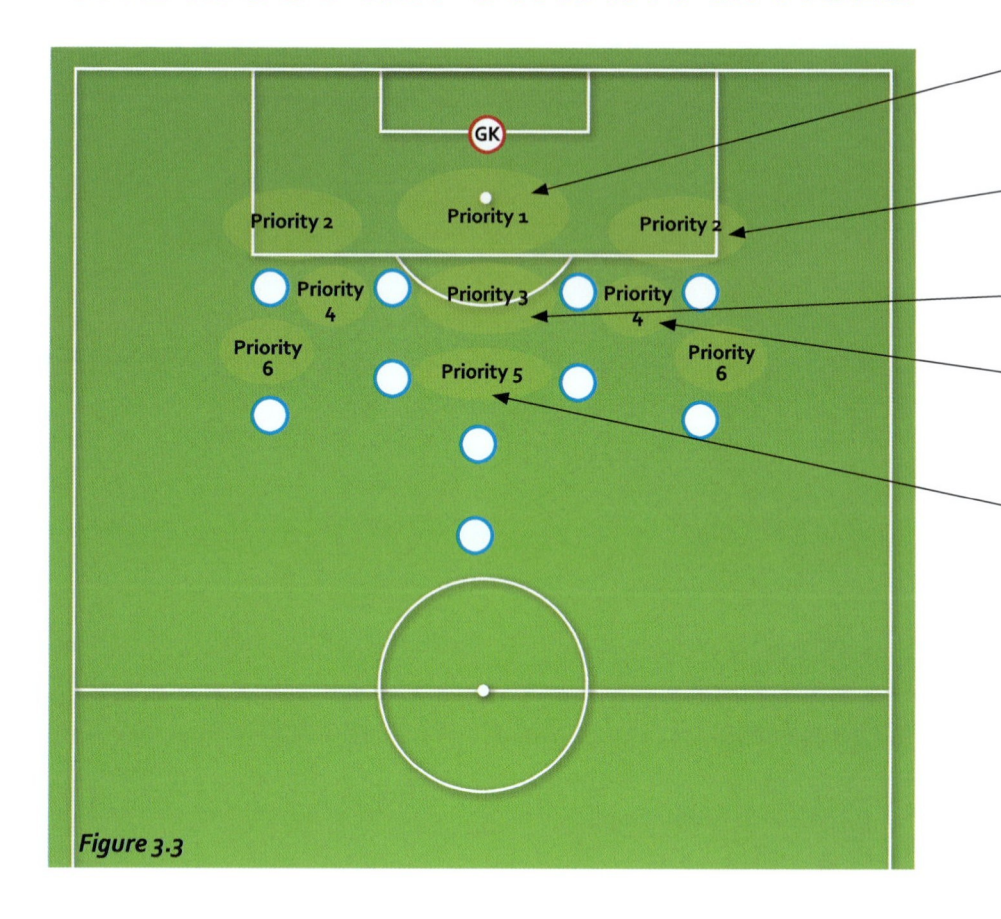

Figure 3.3

For further thinking

How do you reach the most important space according to the Game Model you have?

Where would you like the final pass to come from on a regular basis?

How would you present this to the players prior to a session?

In which way can incorporate this in your game plan?

In which way can you make sure that this principle is not forgotten or de-prioritized - week in and week out?

1st priority should be to get behind the center backs. Can I pass the ball there - or should I go to 2nd priority

2nd priority should be to play the ball into the space behind the fullbacks.

3rd priority would be to get in between the two centerbacks in this case. A prioritized defending area in most cases.

4th priority would be to get in between the center backs and the fullbacks. Is it possible to get there right away? If not - go further down in the hierarchical order.

5th priority would be to get in behind the central midfielders. A perfect space to eventually prioritize option nr 1 - behind the center backs.

This is a version first presented by Josh Faga*, on how to prioritize space in defending as well as attacking. A great way of visualizing spaces and how to make the right priorities when you're attacking. We added the spaces horizontally in between the players - not just the vertical spaces.

*https://www.esdfanalysis.com/match-analysis/objectivity-subjectivity-philosophy-defending/

"VS SPAIN, WORLD CUP 2010"

Implementation Rotations vs Spain World Cup 2010
In this section there will be an array of situations that will be shown graphically, in order to make it structurally easy to follow - and to show how Bielsa has deployed rotations in his past, and how he has done so in certain contexts.

The first example shown, is the World Cup game against Spain back in 2010 in South Africa. Although ultimately losing the game (1-2 to the Champions), there are certain aspects that have caught our attention. Particularly one situation stands out - since we are familiar first hand with part of the preparation which took place ahead of the Mexico-Chile experience.

What Bielsa implemented was in how to deal with the opposing three central midfielders of Spain. With a meticulous preparation and how to get one player available for a pass that bypasses the opponent is a real work of art - but yet comprehendible.

Adaption vs Spain, World Cup 2010 - release of nr 6 (left sided entry)

Instructions:
1. Nr 6 moves to the right to create space
2. Nr 8 moves into the space where nr 6 moved from
3. A potential center back passes the ball to nr 6
4. Nr 6 passes the ball to nr 8
5. Nr 10 moves into space diagonally from nr 8
6. Nr 6 starts to make a diagonal run
7. Nr 8 passes the ball to nr 10
8. Nr 10 passes the ball into the space between the opposite central midfielders

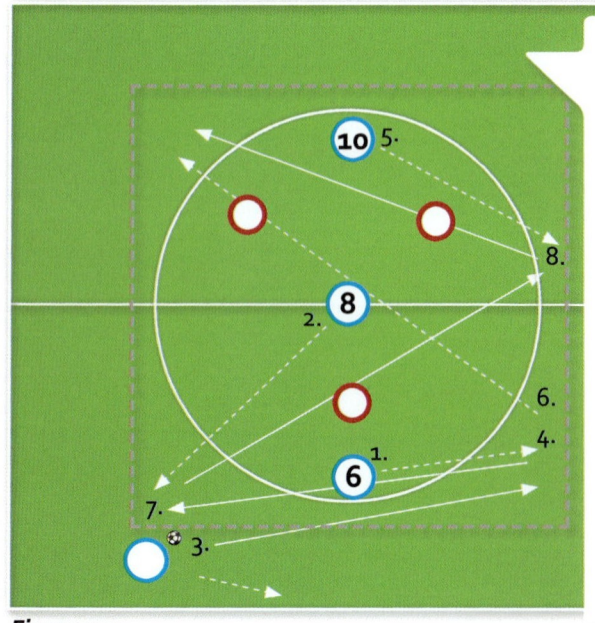

Figure 3.4

Adaption vs Spain, World Cup 2010 - release of nr 6 (right sided entry)

Instructions:
1. Nr 6 moves to the left to create space
2. Nr 8 moves into the space where nr 6 moved from
3. A potential center back passes the ball to nr 6
4. Nr 6 passes the ball to nr 8
5. Nr 10 moves into space diagonally from nr 8
6. Nr 6 starts to make a diagonal run
7. Nr 8 passes the ball to nr 10
8. Nr 10 passes the ball into the space between the opposite central midfielders

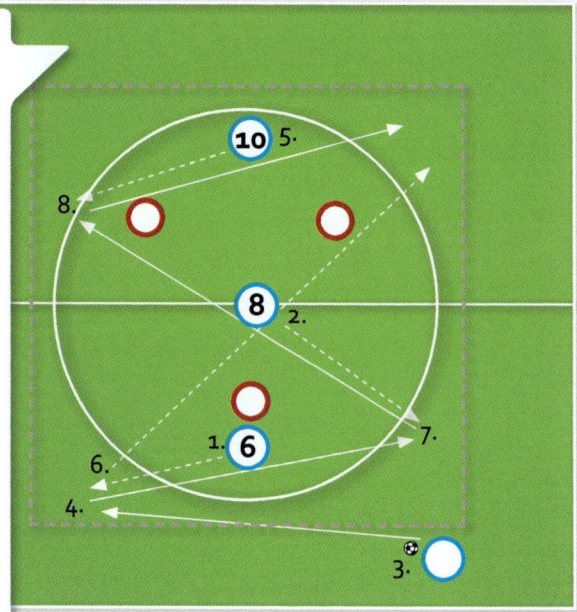

Figure 3.5

Adaption vs Spain, World Cup 2010 - up back through with release of 6 (right)

Instructions:
1. Nr 6 moves to the right to create space
2. Nr 8 moves into the space where nr 6 moved from
3. A potential center back passes the ball to nr 6
4. Nr 10 moves into the diagonal space from nr 6
5. Nr 6 passes the ball to nr 10
6. Nr 10 executes a support pass to nr 8
7. Nr 6 has already started his deep run outside of the opposing midfielder to the right
8. Nr 8 passes the ball into the space between the opposite central midfielders

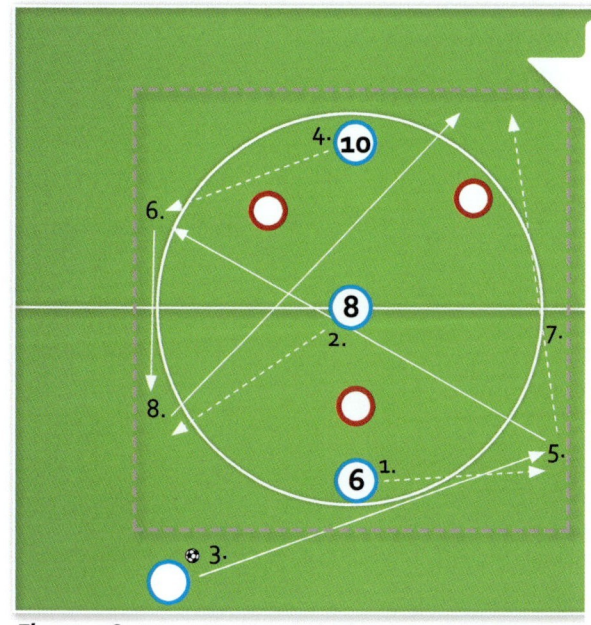

Figure 3.6

41

Adaption vs Spain, World Cup 2010 - up back through with release of 6 (left)

Instructions:
1. Nr 6 moves to the left to create space
2. Nr 8 moves into the space where nr 6 moved from
3. A potential center back passes the ball to nr 6
4. Nr 10 moves into the diagonal space from nr 6
5. Nr 6 passes the ball to nr 10
6. Nr 10 executes a support pass to nr 8
7. Nr 6 has already started his deep run outside of the opposing midfielder to the right
8. Nr 8 passes the ball into the space between the opposite central midfielders

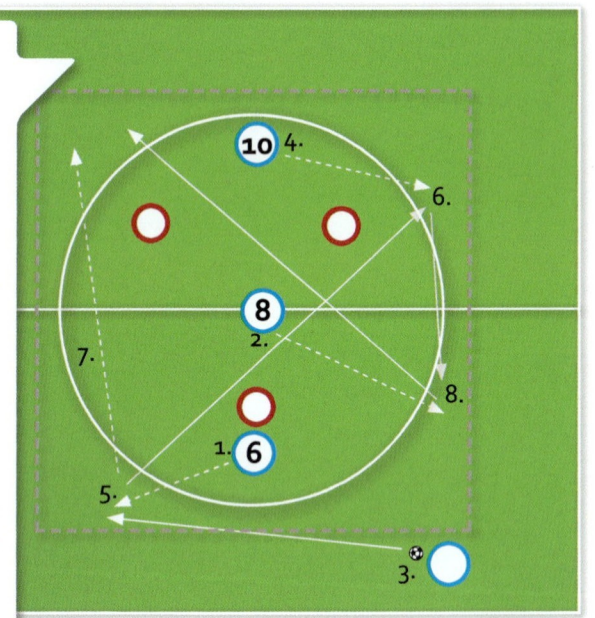

Figure 3.7

The examples as noted are with the release of nr 6 - in order to get the free man available for the pass - which in itself bypasses the opponent - which is rigidly implemented by Bielsa's teams.

Questions for you as a coach: How would you involve a potentially 4th player, which might be a striker? What kind of space would that player occupy or potentially move into to create an even more numerical superiority?

> "*Organization is just a foundation and should never limit you as a coach and your players creativity to create and use space*"
>
> /John Wall

> *"Your job is to serve the players, not the other way around"*

An important lesson that Bielsa is trying to teach us - is that you have to guide and actually implement more levels of your game plan and playing style even to the smallest or tiny detail in training - not just in form of tactical exercises or training games but even down to pattern play - individual talks - video preparations - instructions – detailed coaching pointers.

Further questions:
- How would arrange the same exercise so that nr 8 gets released?
- The same goes for nr 10, how would you arrange that?
- What specific corridor - space do you want to solve or use in order to create a superiority against your opponent?
- How would you create a framework of principles for your players to comprehend reoccurring game situations in build up?

Attacking Phases

Here's an outline on how to structure your Style of Play. And to implement rotations and interchanges you need to ask yourself where could it be possible to adapt and tweak it more to (all in a non-specific order):
- The players (age, experience, background)
- The team (traits, strengths/weaknesses, prioritized spaces)
- The club (external factors, history, philosophy)

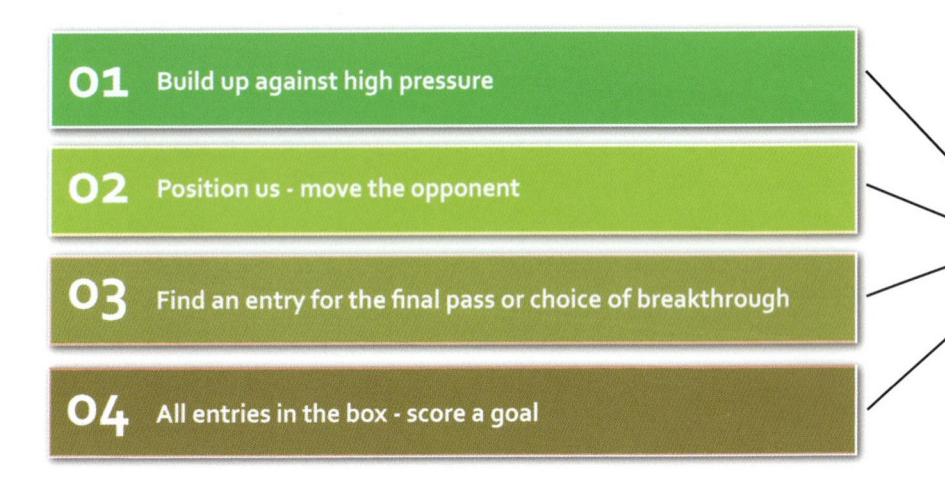

01	Build up against high pressure
02	Position us - move the opponent
03	Find an entry for the final pass or choice of breakthrough
04	All entries in the box - score a goal

All spaces are generally constructed. The phase is obviously affected by where your opponent is. Factors such as time - where did you restart your play from (did you just win the ball, did you just win a free-kick?) Moreover, players need to actually recognize when to bypass one phase in order to move forward towards a possible goal scoring opportunity.

The only constant thing is change - and **IF** can you aid the development of a team that's unpredictable for the opponent - you actually might have something going for you.

A definition of the phases would be O1 and O2 moving into O3 that's the aim of this segment. The phases will be shown in a separate visual (next page). This is based upon an organization of 1-3-3-1-3 and a simplification of that system. We will outline 6 examples on how to release one of the defenders - or one of the midfielders.

Figure 3.8

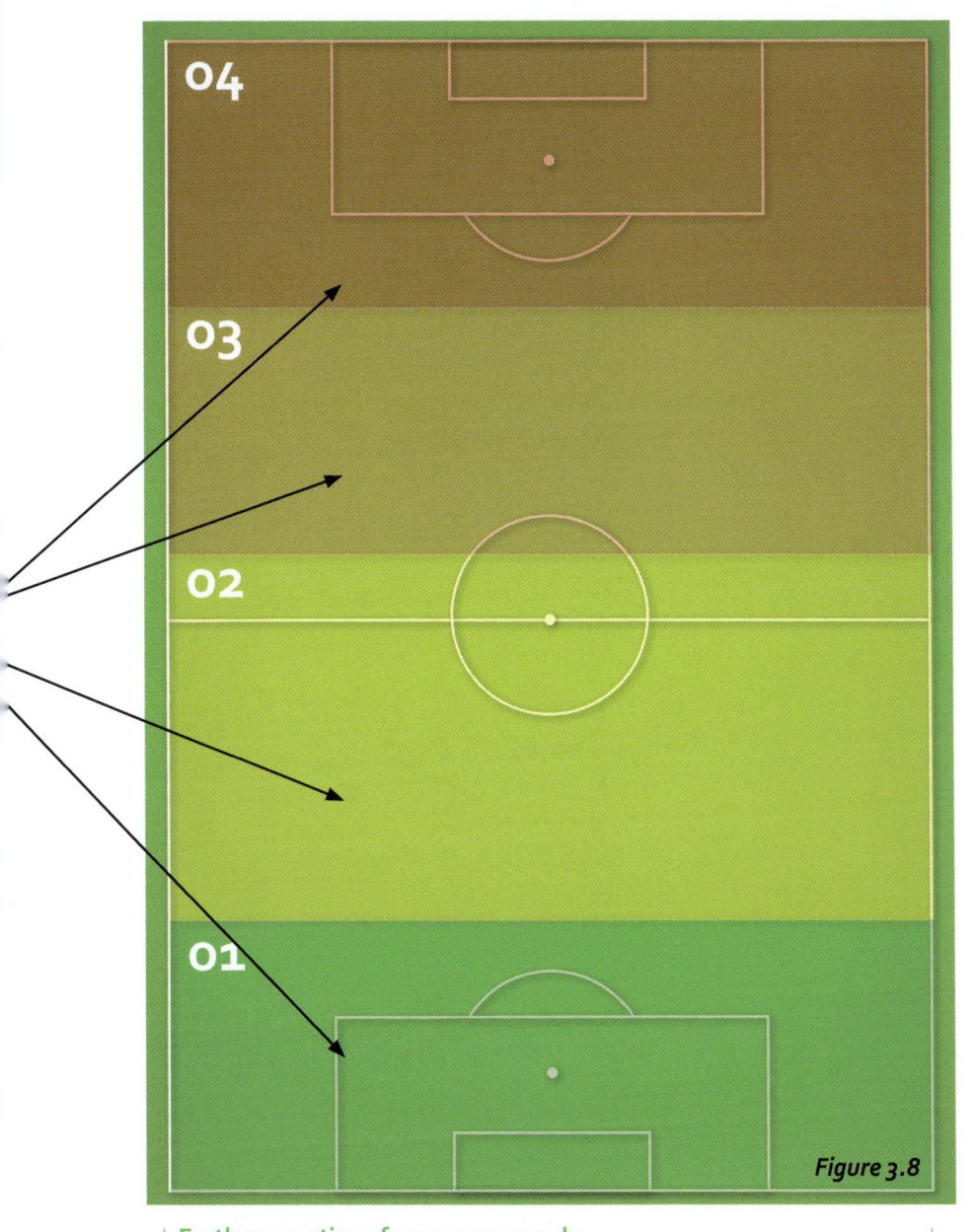

Further questions for you as a coach:

- How can I move the opponent in O2 to successfully release and get one player free?
- What can I do to make it more difficult for the attacking team (role reversal)?
- Can I restart the ball from different positions, and what difference does it make for the exercise?
- How can I manipulate the exercise, so the players actually are doing the desirable decisions?

THE IMPLEMENTATION OF ROTATIONS AGAINST 4-4-2

vs Spain, World Cup 2010

To generalize, the starting positions in a conventional 4-4-2 are pretty standard. What Bielsa fostered was a habit of implementing rotations in build-up and bypassing the opponent consistently and regularly. The term "release" should be looked upon as getting one player free - in order to successfully move further up the pitch.

By using an organization of 1-3-3 vs 4-2 (7v6) the following starting positions would be:

(7v6) starting positions:

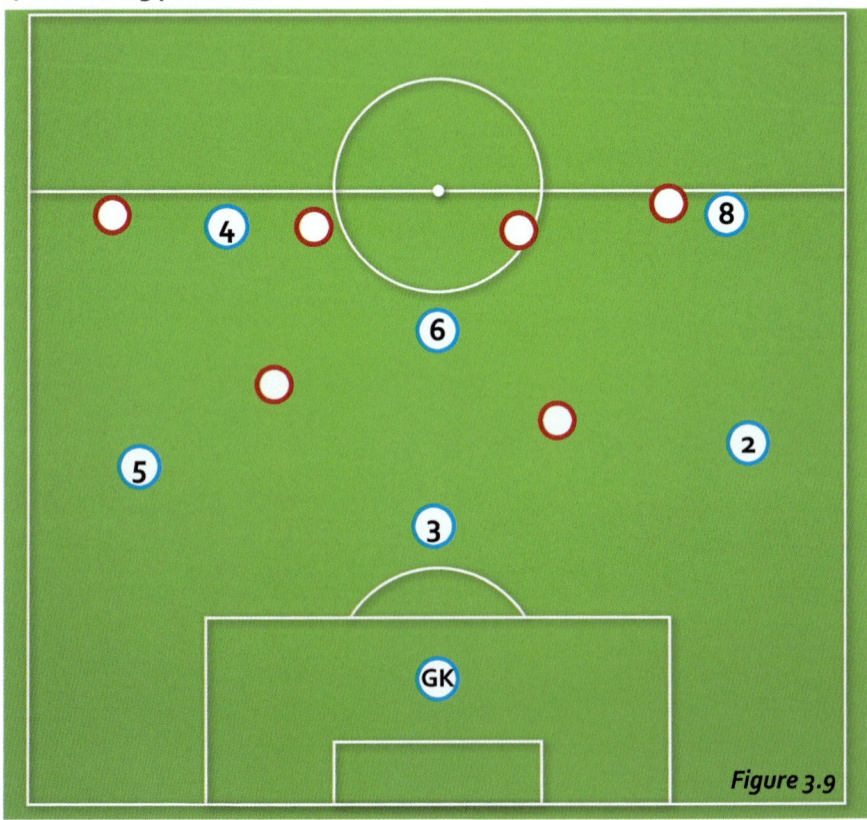

Figure 3.9

Implementations of Rotations, Release player 2 vs 4-4-2

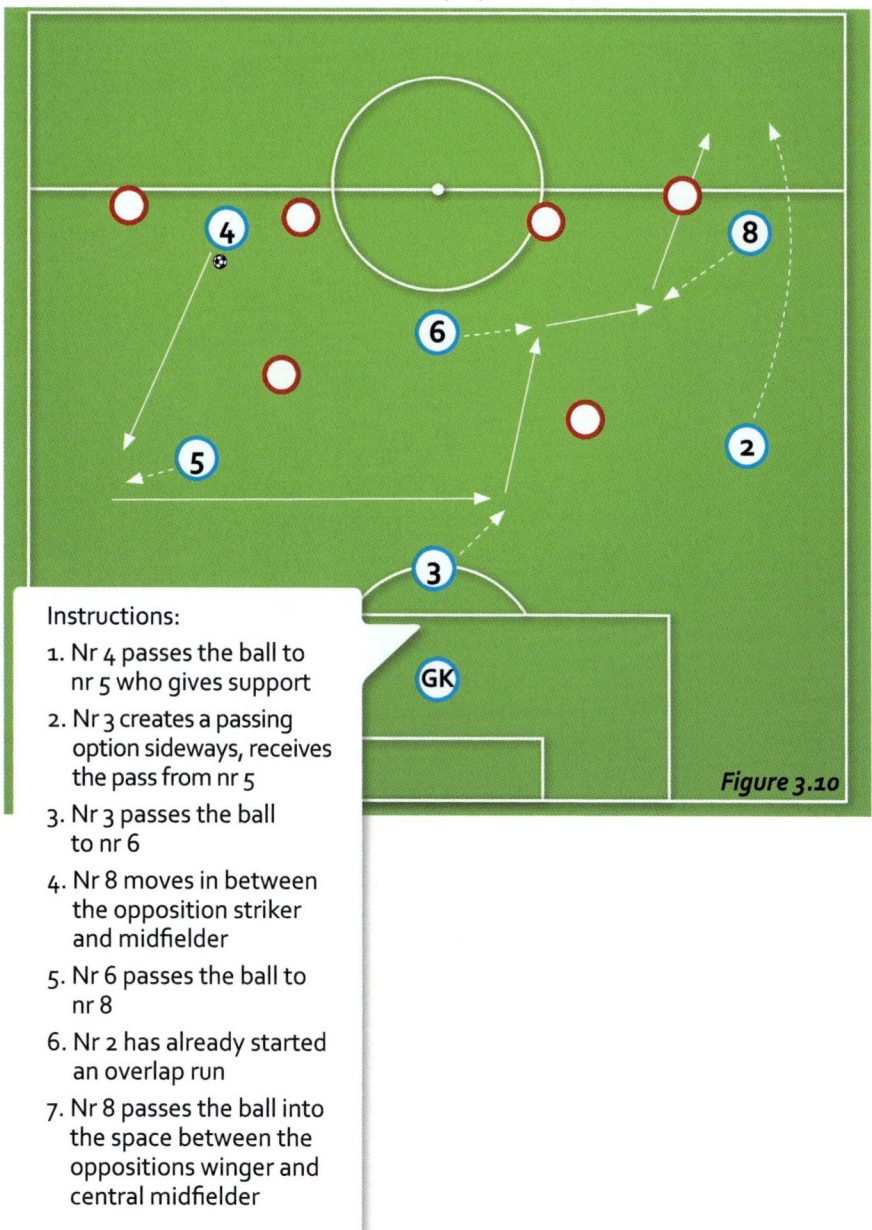

Instructions:
1. Nr 4 passes the ball to nr 5 who gives support
2. Nr 3 creates a passing option sideways, receives the pass from nr 5
3. Nr 3 passes the ball to nr 6
4. Nr 8 moves in between the opposition striker and midfielder
5. Nr 6 passes the ball to nr 8
6. Nr 2 has already started an overlap run
7. Nr 8 passes the ball into the space between the oppositions winger and central midfielder

Figure 3.10

Implementations of Rotations, Release player 8 vs 4-4-2

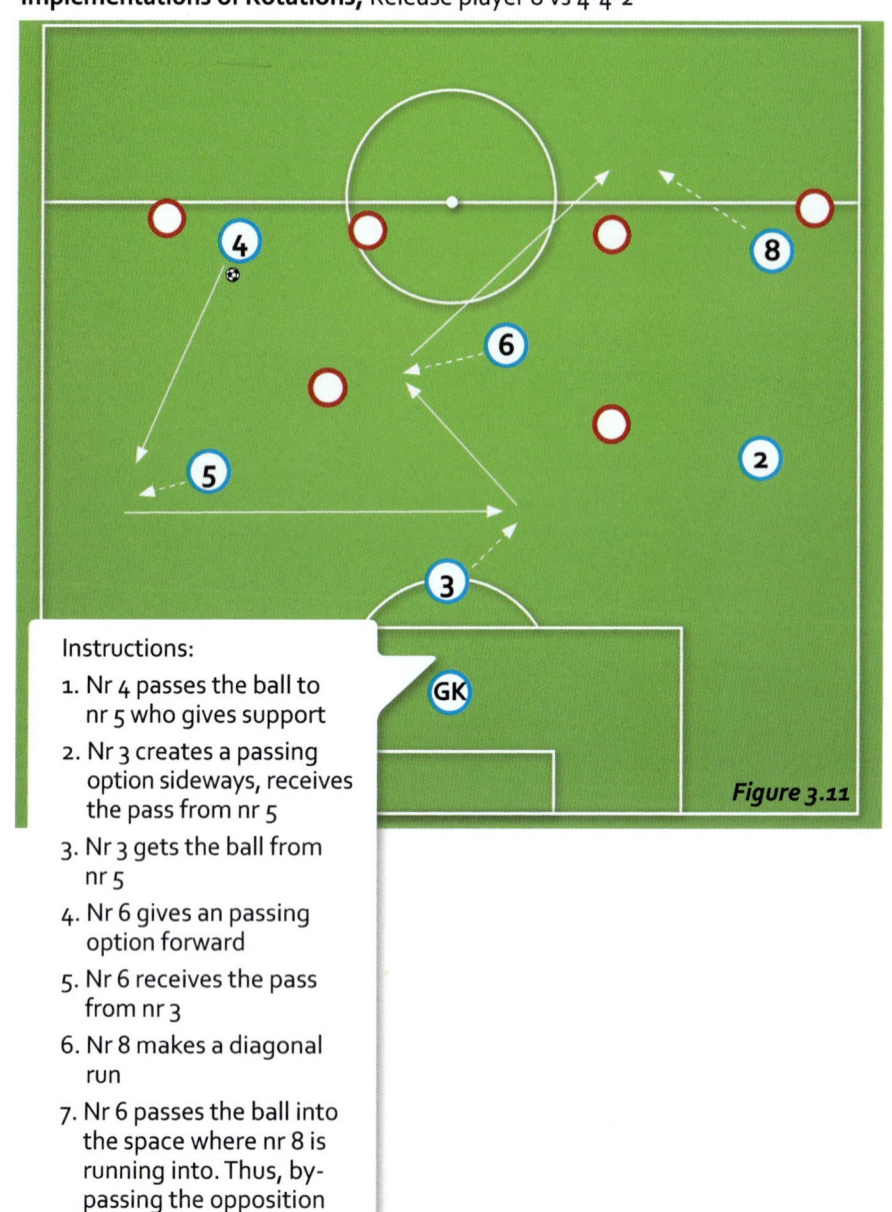

Figure 3.11

Instructions:

1. Nr 4 passes the ball to nr 5 who gives support
2. Nr 3 creates a passing option sideways, receives the pass from nr 5
3. Nr 3 gets the ball from nr 5
4. Nr 6 gives an passing option forward
5. Nr 6 receives the pass from nr 3
6. Nr 8 makes a diagonal run
7. Nr 6 passes the ball into the space where nr 8 is running into. Thus, by-passing the opposition midfield line.

Implementations of Rotations, Release player 2 vs 4-4-2

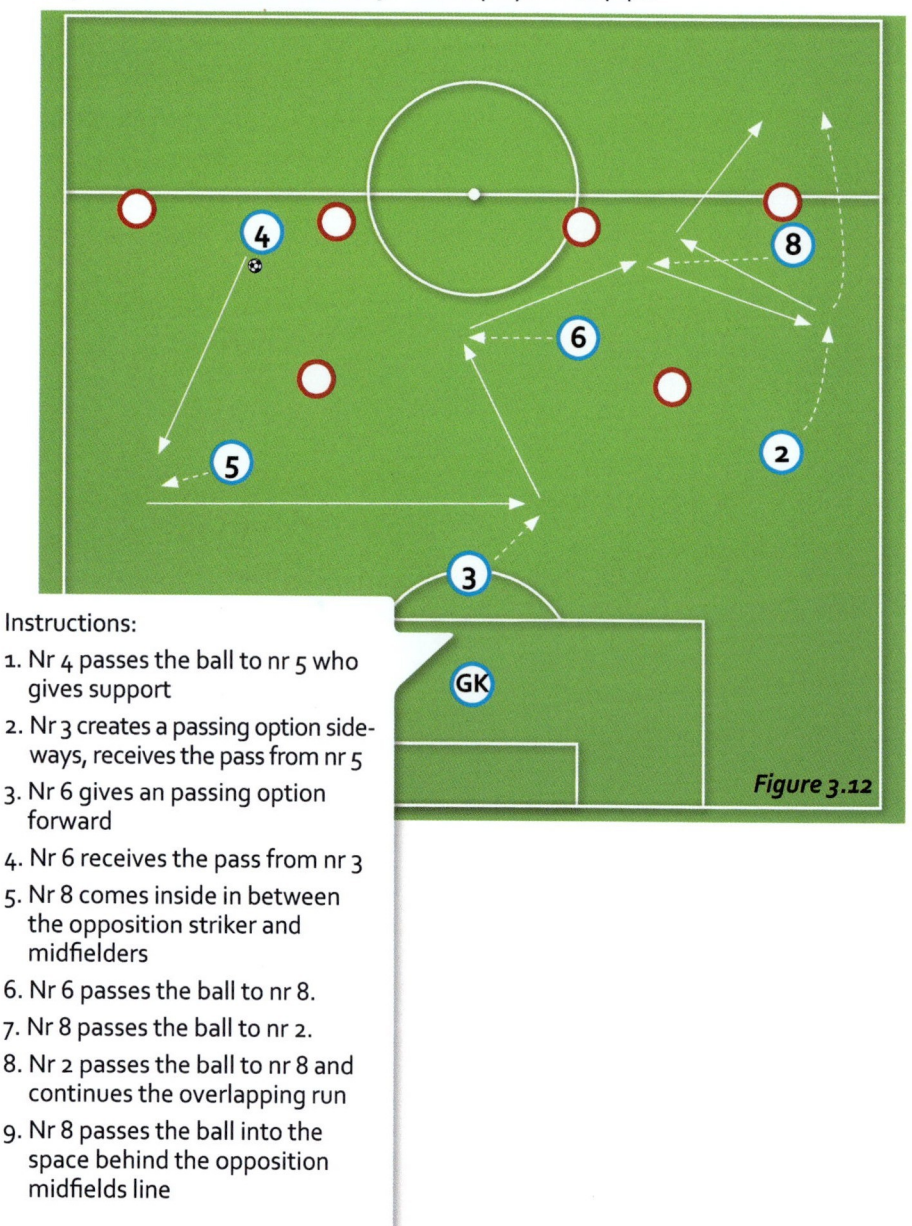

Figure 3.12

Instructions:

1. Nr 4 passes the ball to nr 5 who gives support
2. Nr 3 creates a passing option sideways, receives the pass from nr 5
3. Nr 6 gives an passing option forward
4. Nr 6 receives the pass from nr 3
5. Nr 8 comes inside in between the opposition striker and midfielders
6. Nr 6 passes the ball to nr 8.
7. Nr 8 passes the ball to nr 2.
8. Nr 2 passes the ball to nr 8 and continues the overlapping run
9. Nr 8 passes the ball into the space behind the opposition midfields line

"I WON'T SHARE YOU"
5v3 Rondo

5v3 will be our starting point. Based on the fact we want to illustrate an example when you're only initially playing against one line of defense - therefore you can foster the initial understanding of rotations in a build up (Attacking). The 5v3 is merely a suggestion, but for us it is vital that there is a minimum starting point is 4 players (diamond shape). This covers Forward - Left - Right - Back initially and gives a clear orientation for the players to fill (having 3 passing options continuously).

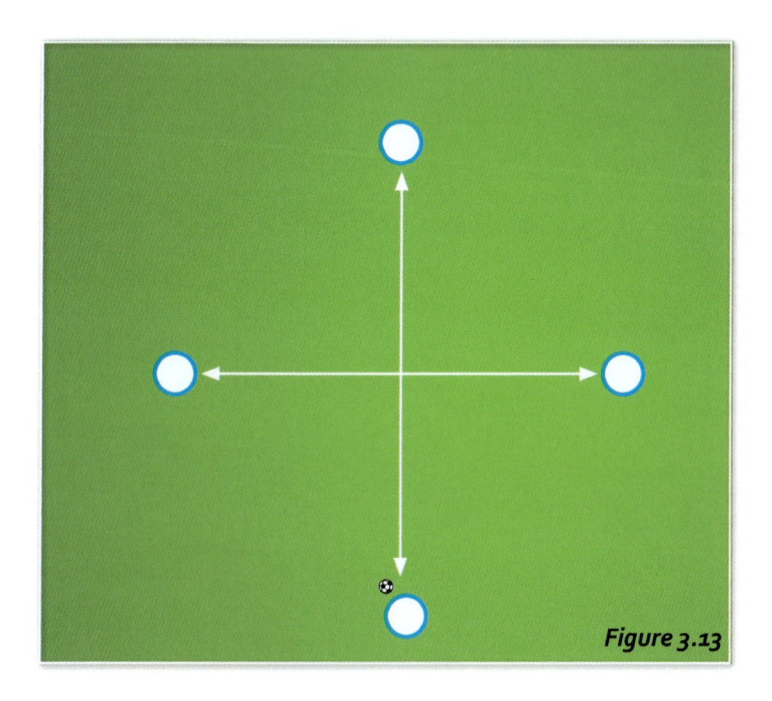

Figure 3.13

The 5th player is the actual central midfielder - 3 lines minimum to play the ball forward (Center back - Midfielder - Left/Right Midfielder - Striker).
- To have 3 players playing against the one line of opponents at least creates initial questions right away
- How can I together with my teammates create an opportunity to bypass the opponent with as many as possible involved

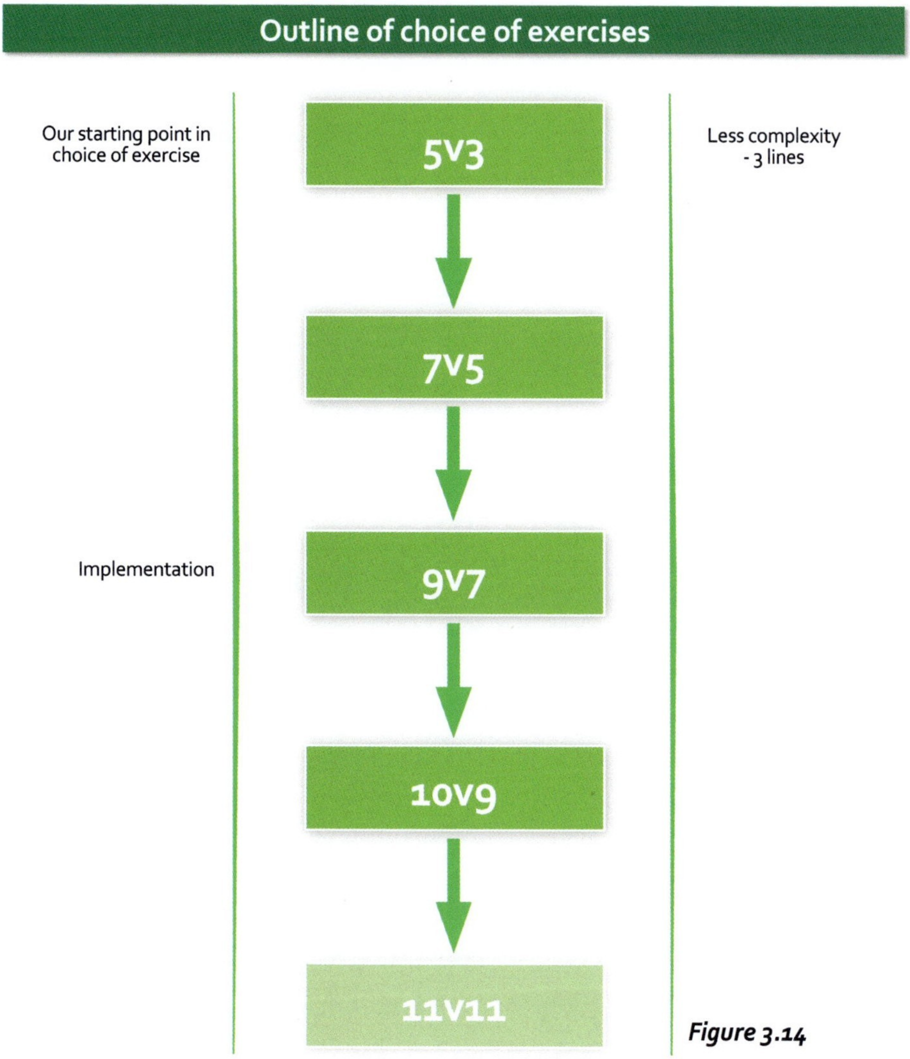

Outline of choice of exercises

Our starting point in choice of exercise

5v3

↓

7v5

↓

Implementation

9v7

↓

10v9

↓

11v11

Less complexity
- 3 lines

Figure 3.14

"A RUSH AND A PUSH AND THE LAND IS OURS"

What: 5v3 (5 offensive players against 3 defending players)

Why: Introduction to rotations and simplification of method in Build Up

How: Set up a rondo and try to adapt to your playing organization

Coaching Points:
- How to create space together - not independently
- After a pass, quickly be available to receive a pass in a new space
- Make use of the whole space (vertical - horizontally)
- Move the opposition by waiting and timing (manipulate the opposition)
- Positions (is it perhaps a center back playing with 3 central midfielders and a striker?)
- Primarily coach the movement of the players without the ball
- What is a probable next scenario after a pass from the center back? Ask the players
- Position-Moment-Direction-Speed is applicable to correct players and create a more direct understanding in what you want to achieve in your coaching*

Recommendations:
- We have not given the dimensions of the exercise - because that is your job as a coach to decide
- Bigger size - slower tempo - but better to get an understanding of the exercise and what the ultimate intention is with respect to your playing style
- 5v3 is a recommendation - but it can also mean 6v3 because it suits you and your players better
- You can be even more specific in your instructions to certain players - depending on your playing style
- You can create a realistic scenario no matter your organization. Try to fill up the field space with different rondos
- Set demands!

5v3 Rondo

Basic Setup of the Exercise (Rondo)

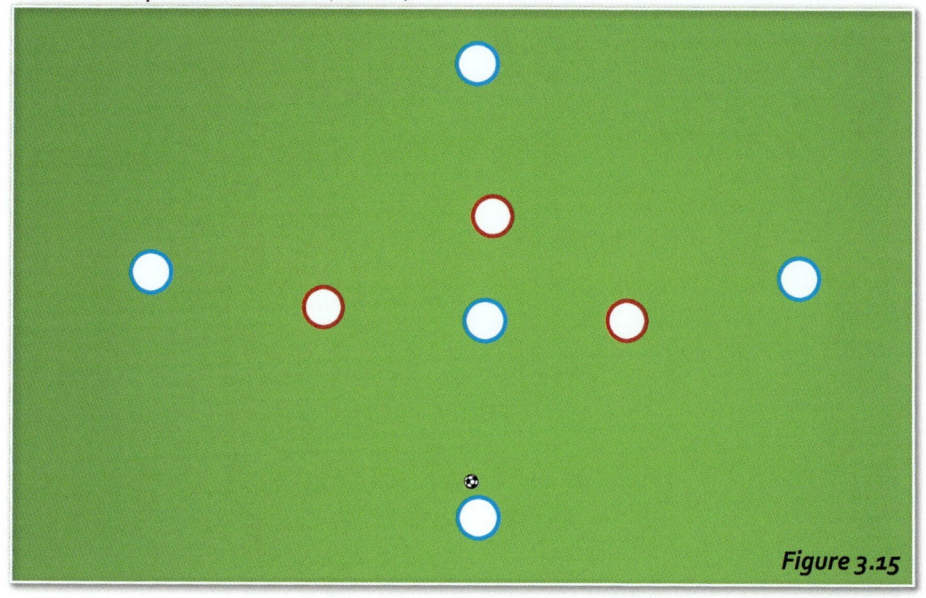

Figure 3.15

One example of a rotation (horizontal).

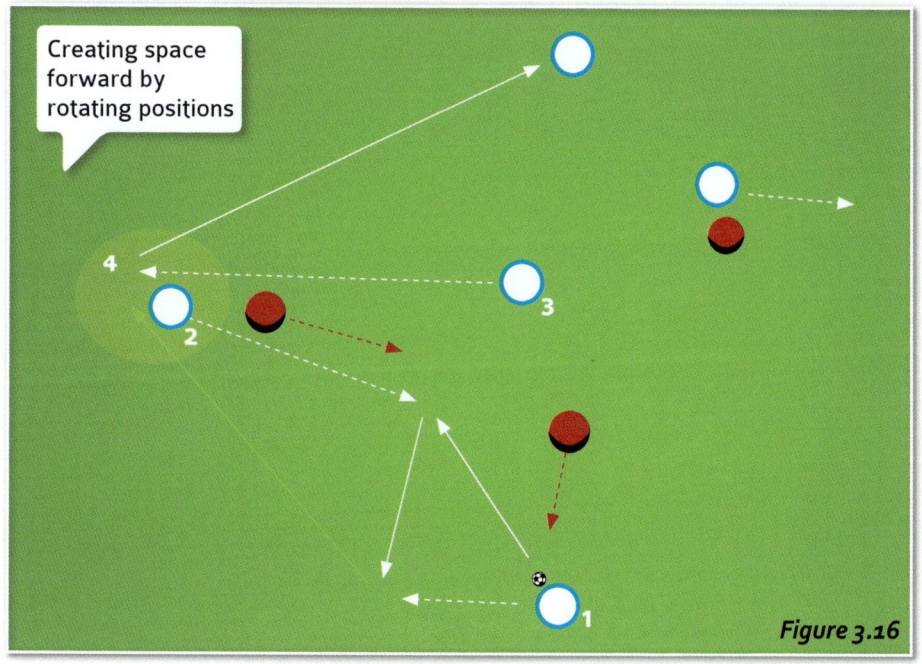

Creating space forward by rotating positions

Figure 3.16

*Verheijen, R Periodisation in Football p. 42 World Football Academy

Rotation, 5v3

5V3, Example of a combination of vertical and horizontal rotation

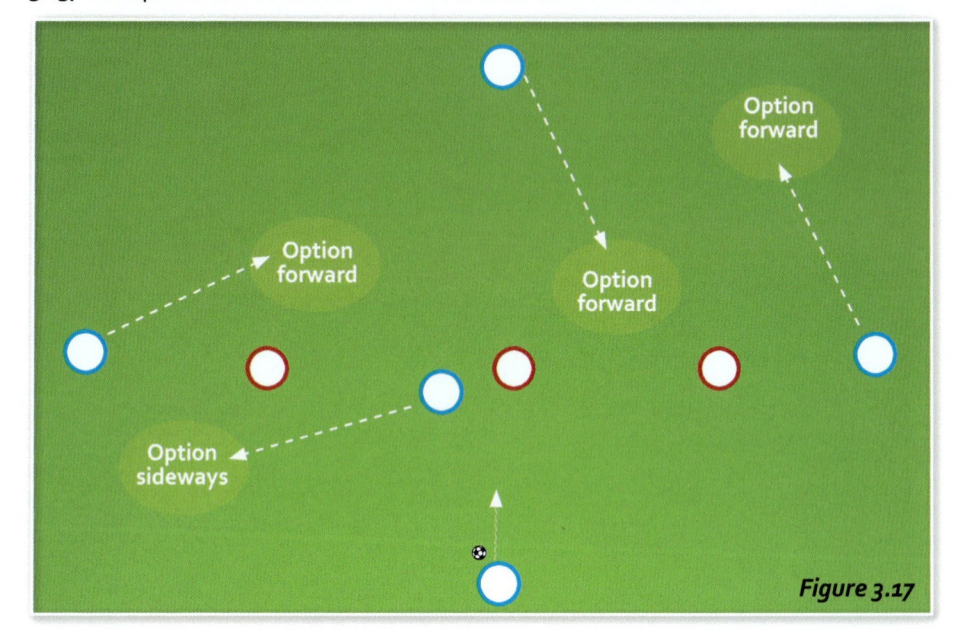

Figure 3.17

Rotation, 5v3

5V3, Example of vertical rotation. Creates space behind the opponents.

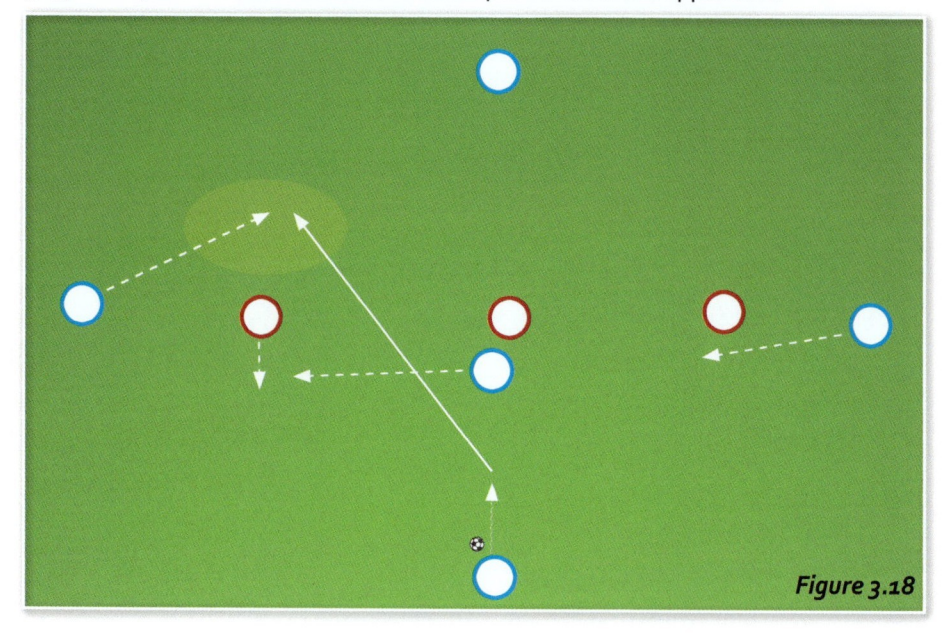

Figure 3.18

"THE HEADMASTERS RITUAL"

What: 7v5 (7 offensive players against 5 defending players)

Why: Progression in application of rotations and simplification of method in Build Up

How: Set up a rondo and try to adapt to your playing organization

Coaching Points:
- How to create space in relationship to each other (above the ball)
- Make use of the whole space (vertical - horizontally)
- Move the opposition by waiting (manipulate the opposition)
- Address to the players to think about the next situation, how do they want it to look
- Primarily coach the movement of the players without the ball
- Position-Timing-Direction-Speed is applicable to correct players and create a more direct understanding in what you want to achieve in your coaching*

Recommendations:
- We have not given the size of the exercise - because this is your decision as a coach to do
- Bigger size - slower tempo - but better to get an understanding of the exercise and what the intention is for your playing style
- 7v5 is a recommendation - but it can also be 7v4 because of training context
- You can be even more specific in your instructions to certain players - depending on your playing style
- You can create a realistic scenario no matter what your organization is. Try to fill up the field space with different rondos
- Set demands!

7v5 Rondo

Starting positions

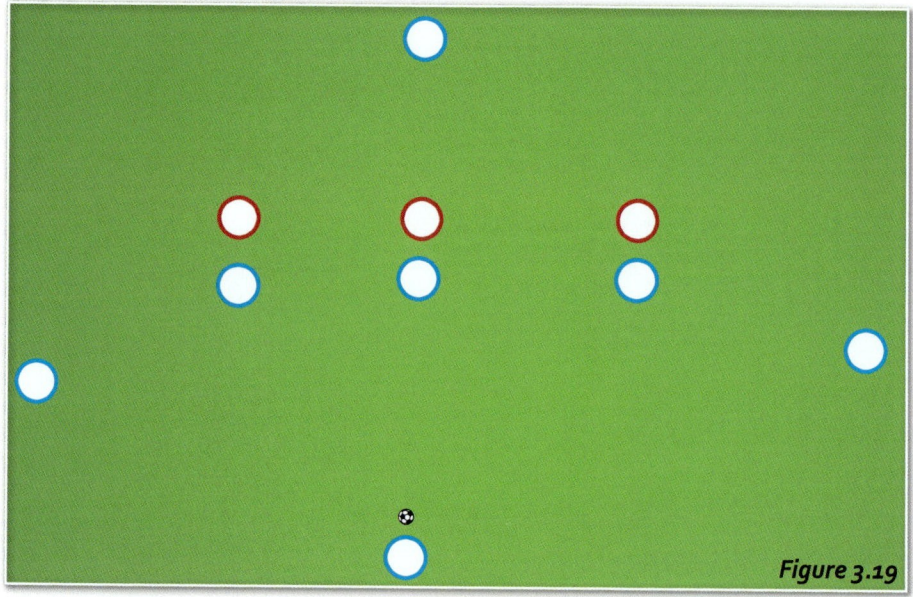

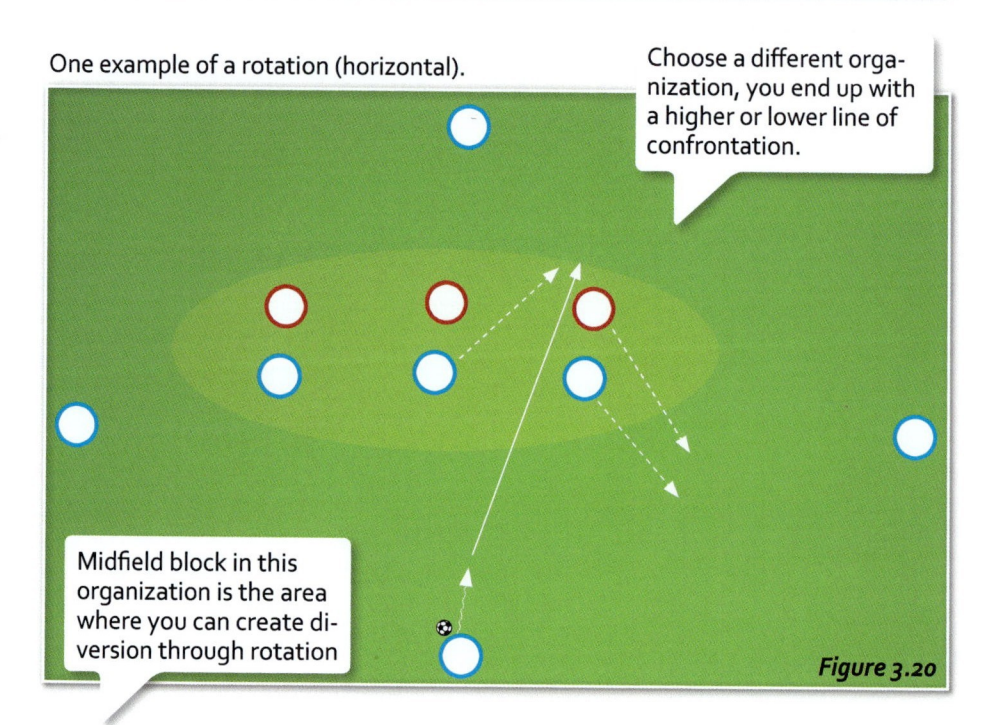

Figure 3.19

One example of a rotation (horizontal).

Choose a different organization, you end up with a higher or lower line of confrontation.

Midfield block in this organization is the area where you can create diversion through rotation

Figure 3.20

*Verheijen, R Periodisation in Football p. 42 World Football Academy

Rotation, 7v5

7V5 - Example of vertical rotation

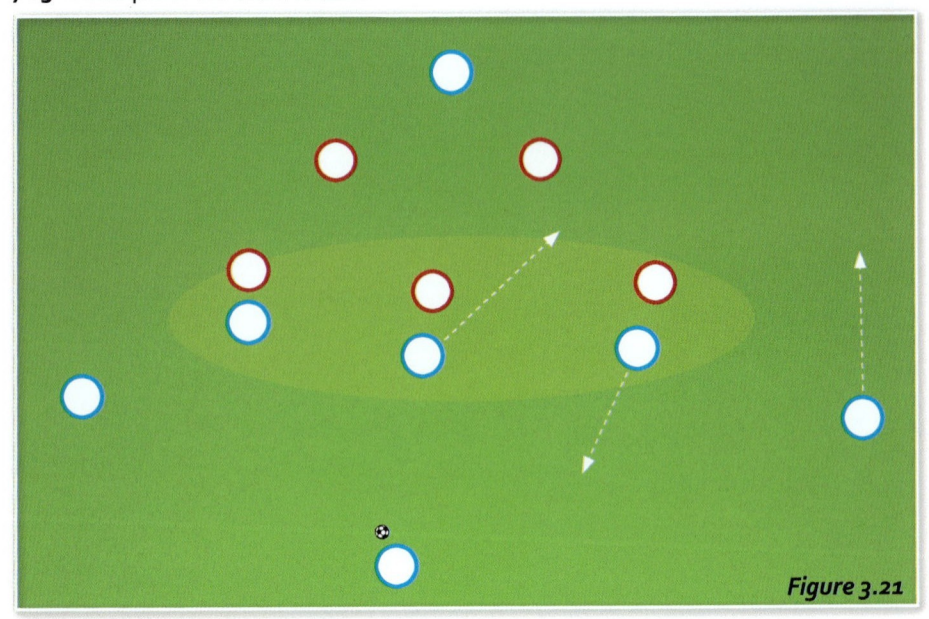

Figure 3.21

7V5 - Example of horizontal rotation

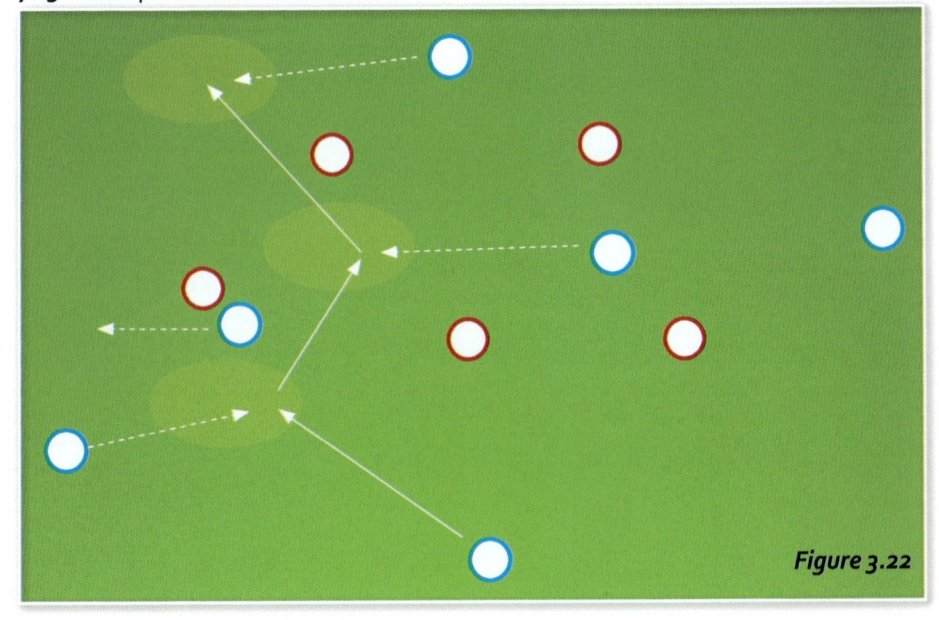

Figure 3.22

Rotation, 7v5

7V5 - Example of vertical and horizontal rotation

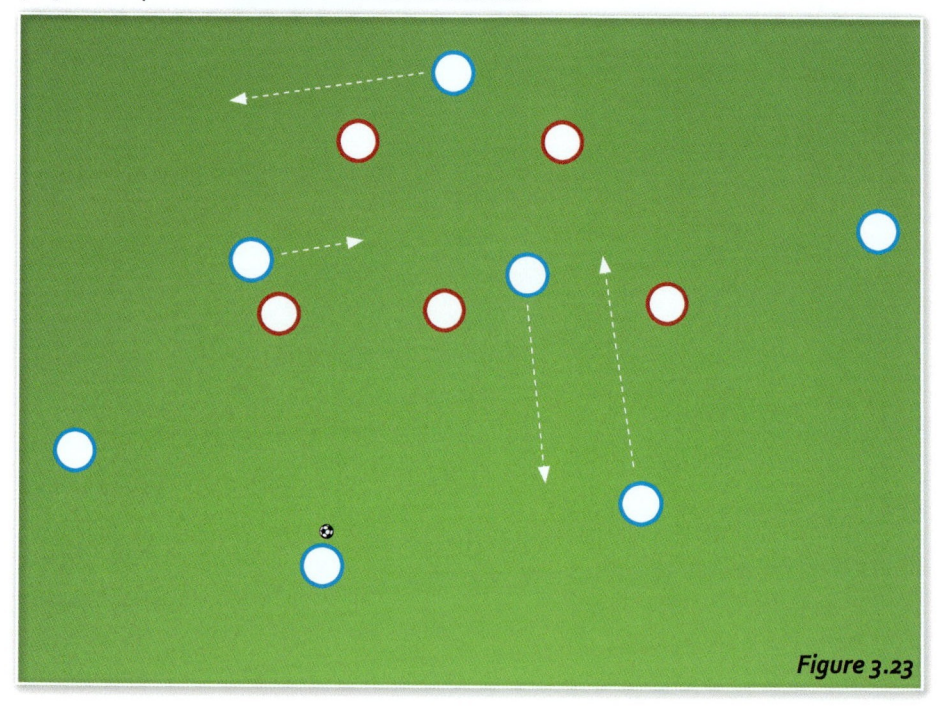

Figure 3.23

"DEATH OF A DISCO DANCER"

What: 9v7 (9 offensive players against 7 defending players)
Why: Progression in application of rotations and simplification of method in Build Up
How: Set up as suggested on the first picture

Coaching Points:
- Coach the opposing team (defending) to cause the higher number team problems
- Coach the next action of players (where to create space after a pass)
- Make use of the whole space (vertical - horizontally)
- Coach the movement of the players without the ball - they create the options for the player with the ball
- A possible next scenario after a successful pass forward: Creating an even better entry
- Position-Timing-Direction-Speed is applicable to correct players and create a more direct understanding in what you want to achieve in your coaching*
- How do we act when we have passed the ball?

Recommendations:
- We have not given the size of the exercise - because that is your decision as a coach to take
- Bigger size - slower tempo - but better to get an understanding of the exercise and what the ultimate intention is with respect for your playing style
- 9v7 is a recommendation - but it can also mean 9v6 because it suits your players better in a context
- You can be even more specific in your instructions to certain players - depending on your playing style
- You can create a realistic scenario no matter what your organization looks like. Try to fill up the field space with different rondos
- Set demands!

9v7 Rondo

Setup and view of corridors

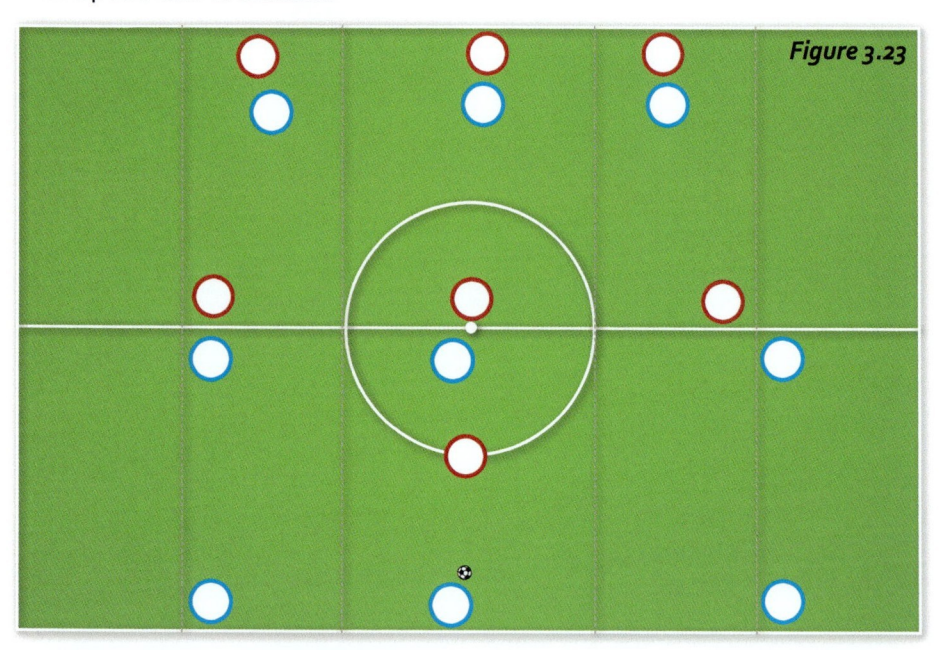

Figure 3.23

Vertical + Horizontal Rotation to create space

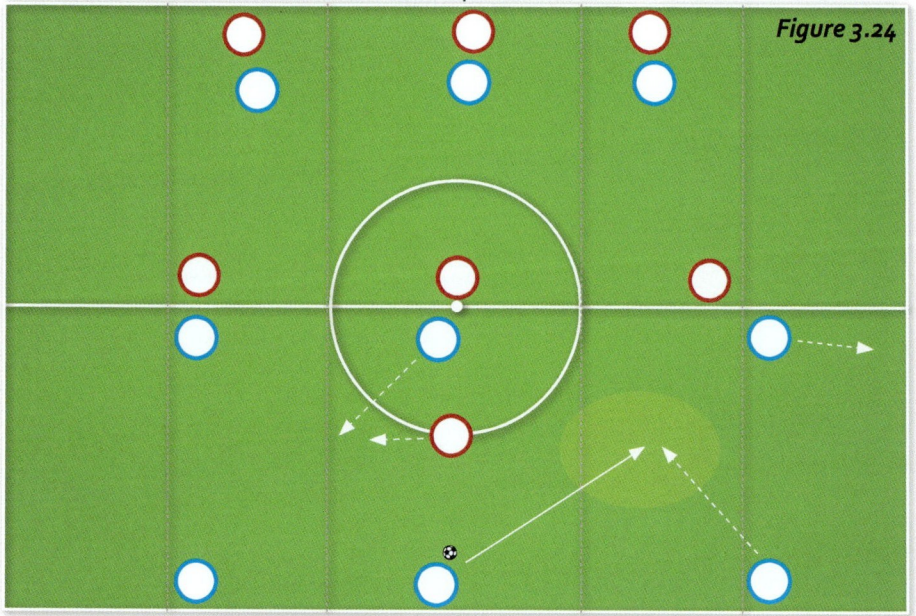

Figure 3.24

*Verheijen, R Periodisation in Football p. 42 World Football Academy

Rotation, 9v7

9V7 - Example of horizontal rotation

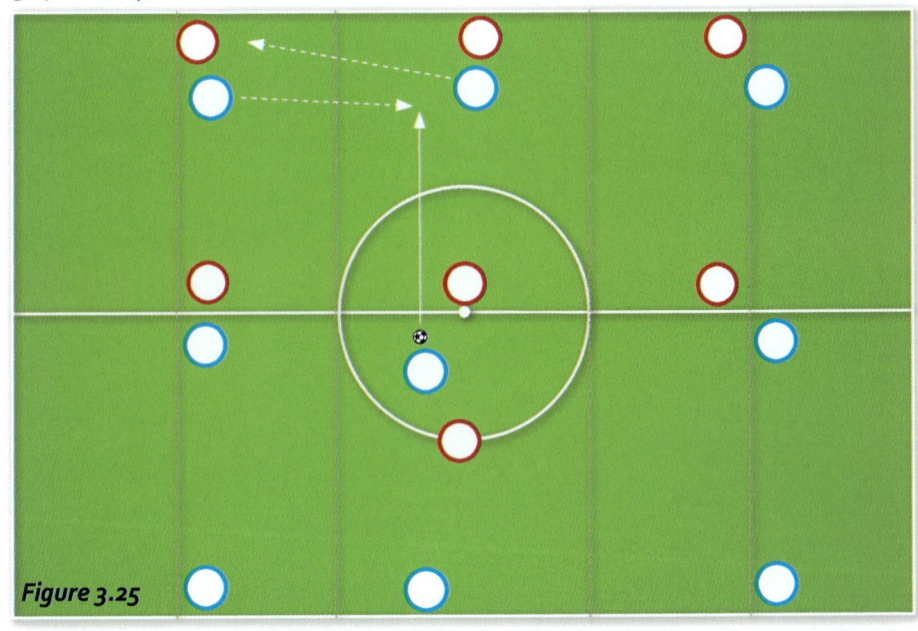

Figure 3.25

Rotation, 9v7

9V7 - Example of vertical rotation

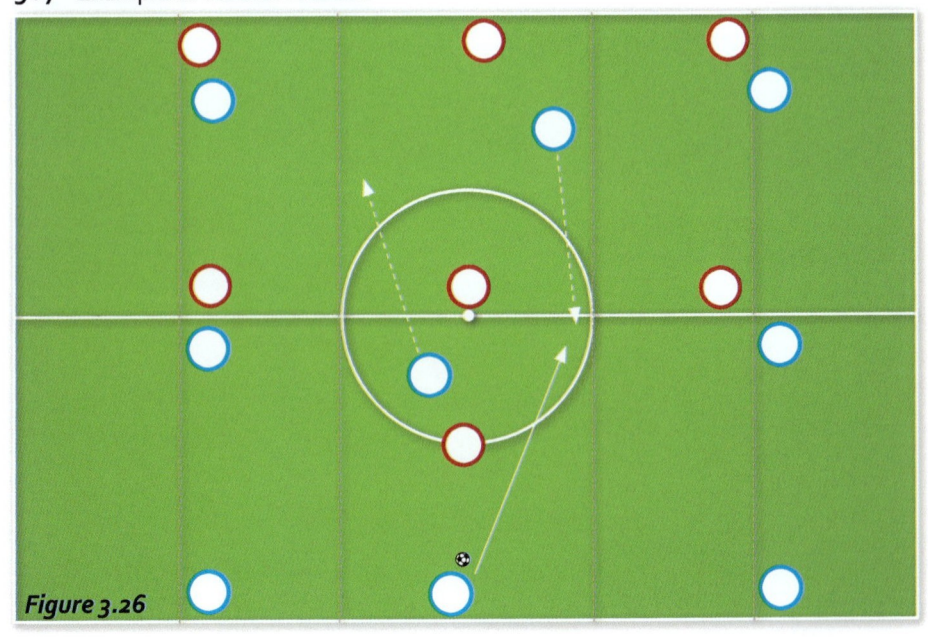

Figure 3.26

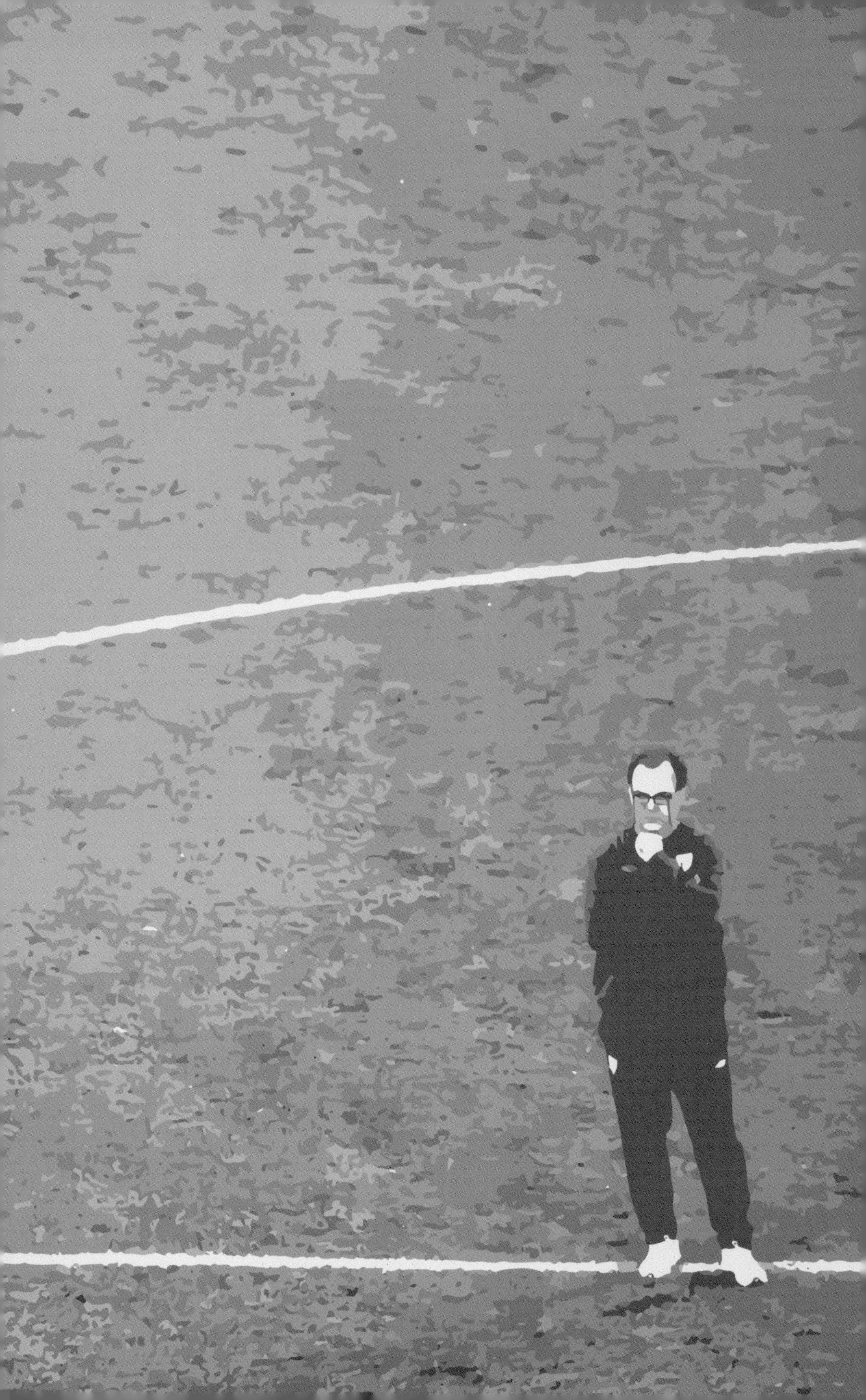

"PAINT A VULGAR PICTURE"

What: 10v9 (10 offensive players against 9 defending players)

Why: Introduction to rotations and simplification of method in Build Up

How: Set up as suggested on the first picture

Coaching Points:

- Coach the opposing team (defending) to cause the higher number team problems
- Coach the next action of players (where to create space after a pass)
- Make use of the whole space (vertical - horizontally)
- How to create
- Coach the movement of the players without the ball - they create the options for the player with the ball
- A possible next scenario after a successful pass forward: How to create an even better entry
- Position-Timing-Direction-Speed is applicable to correct players and create a more direct understanding in what you want to achieve in your coaching*

Recommendations:

- We have not given the size of the exercise - because that is your decision as a coach to take
- Bigger size - slower tempo - but better to get an understanding of the exercise and what the ultimate intention is with respect for your playing style
- 10v9 is a recommendation - but it can also mean 11v8 because it suits your players better in a context
- You can be even more specific in your instructions to certain players - depending on your playing style
- You can create a realistic scenario no matter what your organization looks like. Try to fill up the field space with different rondos
- Set demands!

Picture of 10v9

Setup and view of corridors

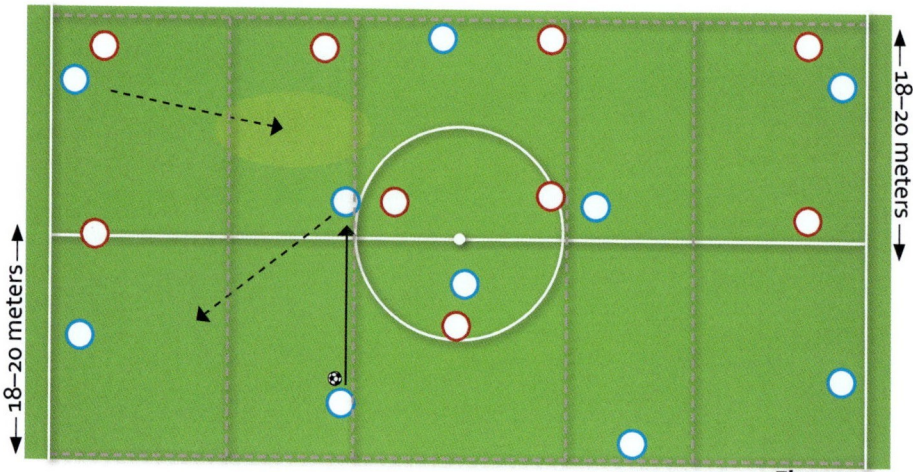

←18–20 meters→

←18–20 meters→

Figure 3.27

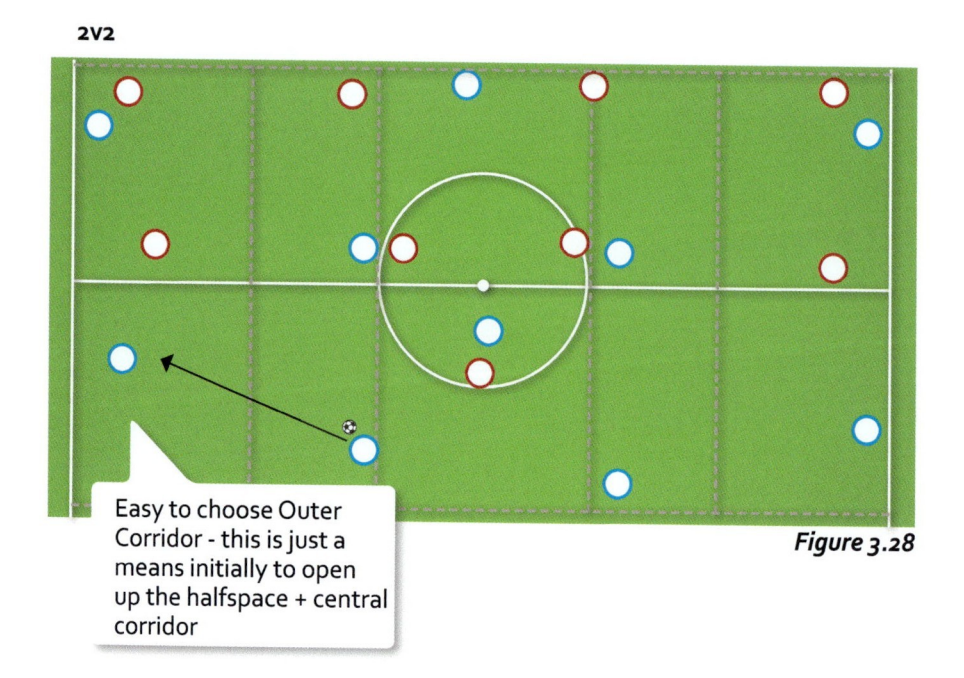

2V2

Easy to choose Outer Corridor - this is just a means initially to open up the halfspace + central corridor

Figure 3.28

*Verheijen, R Periodisation in Football p. 42 World Football Academy

Rotation, 10v9

10v9 - Example of horizontal rotation

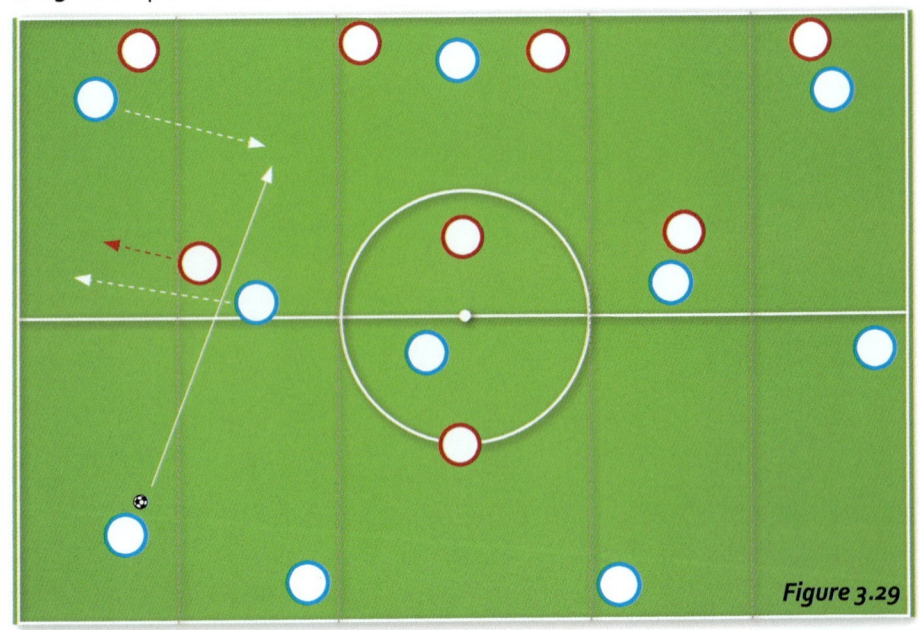

Figure 3.29

Rotation, 10v9

10v9 - Example of vertical rotation

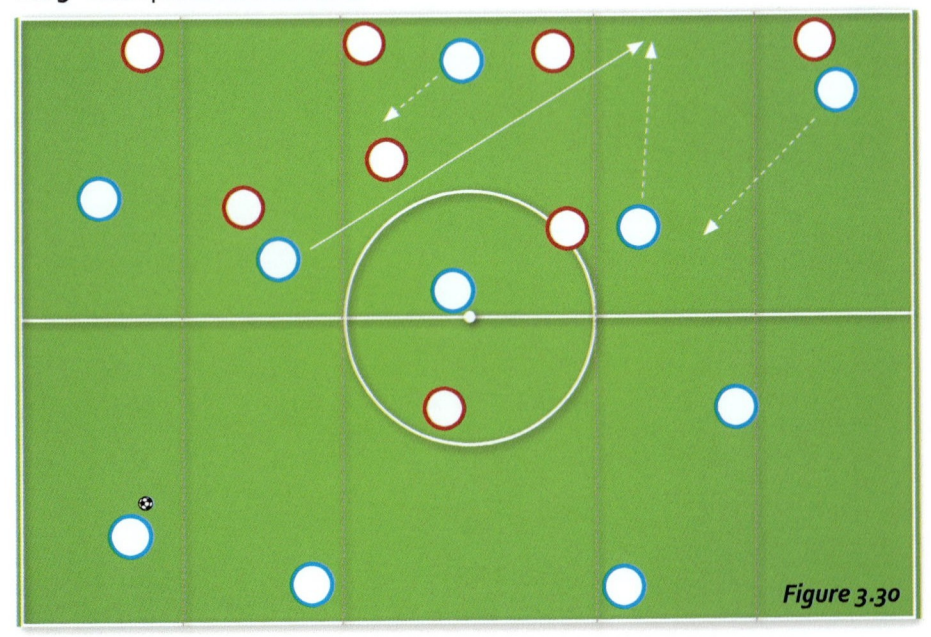

Figure 3.30

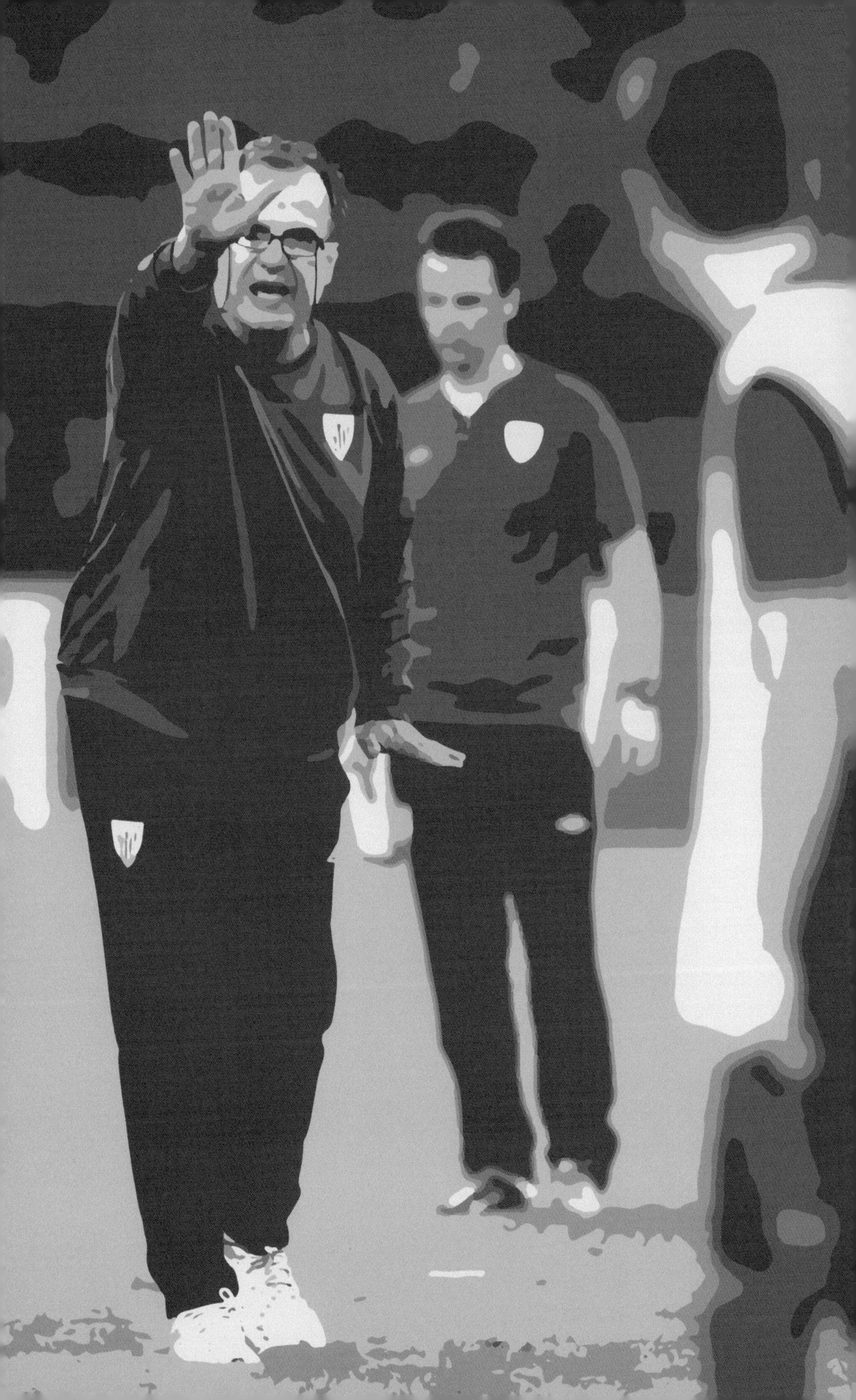

04 SUMMARY

"Pave the way for your players"

Our aim of is to open an array of possibilities for you as a coach to grow and broaden your horizon. Rotations as a form to create a common ground and shared experience - that you in a way already know what's going to happen (and the opponent knows less). As well as a culture, with certain set of shared values, beliefs and quiet agreements - there should be occasions where you are predictable for your teammates and unpredictable for your opponents.

It could also be that creativity could only be allowed if you actually master (or at least know) the script. From a team starting point: You should review and try to follow this logical structure when working with your team:

How to collaborate efficiently
(2v1, 2v2, 3v2 etc.)

Objective Principles
(Creating space for the player with the ball)

Subjective Principles of the Team
(Your Team's traits and your preferred style of Attacking - Transitioning - Defending)

Organization/Role
(A players role within your team's organization, for example 1-4-3-3)

The constant questions should always be there - and things will never reach finality, it has to be repeated, you have to do it wrong - and then get it right, progress and at times question yourself. But you need to love it - and really appreciate that the price is the process, not the destination. And by being logical - try to make very evident why you handle them in specific and certain way - especially for your players. In this way you will gain trust - and try to incorporate the big E's55 every now and then with your players.

Getting back to the outline of this chapter - we have shown a method and a way of dealing with Attack - Build Up. By doing so - we wanted to create a way of how to look on things - but rest assure - not **THE WAY**. What's occurring is the Time - Space constraint and the opponent besides your teammates - how can you deal with them favorably for you and your team.

In order to pave the way for your players - and in a way yourself as well - start with lesser numbers in order to move forward. Knowledge should be attainable but still challenging, and there lies the challenge for you and your players. Take in the suggestions about Cause-Effect thinking - How to think when creating an Exercise - and the logical structure on how to look on your team.

With that being said - best of luck and you need to figure out how make use of these ideas. And please do try to sort the material and put it in within the objective parameters and right after that - into you own reality and your own external factors.

> *How many players that are occupying space in a vertical sense speaks more about what intention they have, whereas the horizontal position reflects more what phase they're in*

INTERC

HANGES

05 INTERCHANGES IN THE FINAL THIRD

"*Bigmouth Strikes Again*"

Introduction
We make a clear distinction between rotation and interchanges - whereas we use Rotation in the Build Up - and Interchanges as the final stages before the eventual Scoring (Creating Goalscoring Chance/s).

A foundation has been laid out, which fosters more discussion of Cooperation, Objective Principles and Subjective Principles as more relevant in-game than (for example) how you organize your team and creating roles for your players.

To avoid unnecessary hiccups when certain situations arise or happen in-game - we are more "no-excuses" types of people. And especially in the case, when you're on the verge of creating a goalscoring chance.
If the cognitive process which we would like to label as Game Insight is as follows:

Recognize - Interpret - Anticipate - Estimate - Judge*
This is where interchanges are, where we can create a common and recognizable situation - where the training process will aid the interpretation - anticipation - estimation and judgement in order to create more positive entries.

*Football Theory World Football Academy (page 37), Tamboer, Jan W.I, Lingen Bert, Verheijen Raymond

When the game is over – it is more likely that the team which creates more (and better) entries into the Golden Zone or penalty box wins the game. And that is exactly where your performance in your role as a coach comes in- how can you aid your team to succeed more with the thing that matters most?

To score one goal more than the opponent
Therefore, as a logical consequence we have now arrived at the very subject - Creating positive entries into the box. Make it as part of your own style of play - understood by everyone and executed in such a high tempo that the opponents don't really have an answer for how to deal with it. We have laid focus on the 3 central corridors (Left Halfspace - Central Corridor - Right Halfspace). The possible combinations are endless - we will give you some examples as a foundation, the rest will be up to you.

> *Something viewed as timing is just a fragment of what really is going on.*

Methodology
And as with everything - find your way. Know your players. Inspire them. Teach them. Guide them. Put high demands on them. Make sure that their strengths will be put to good use for the team.

Interchange

Method

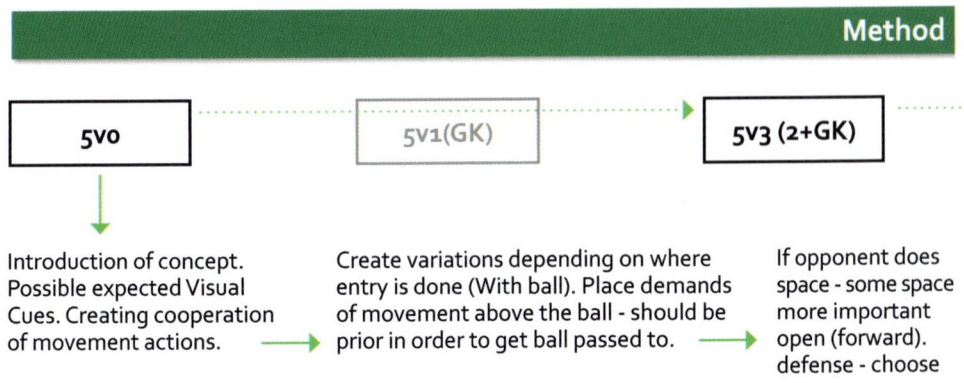

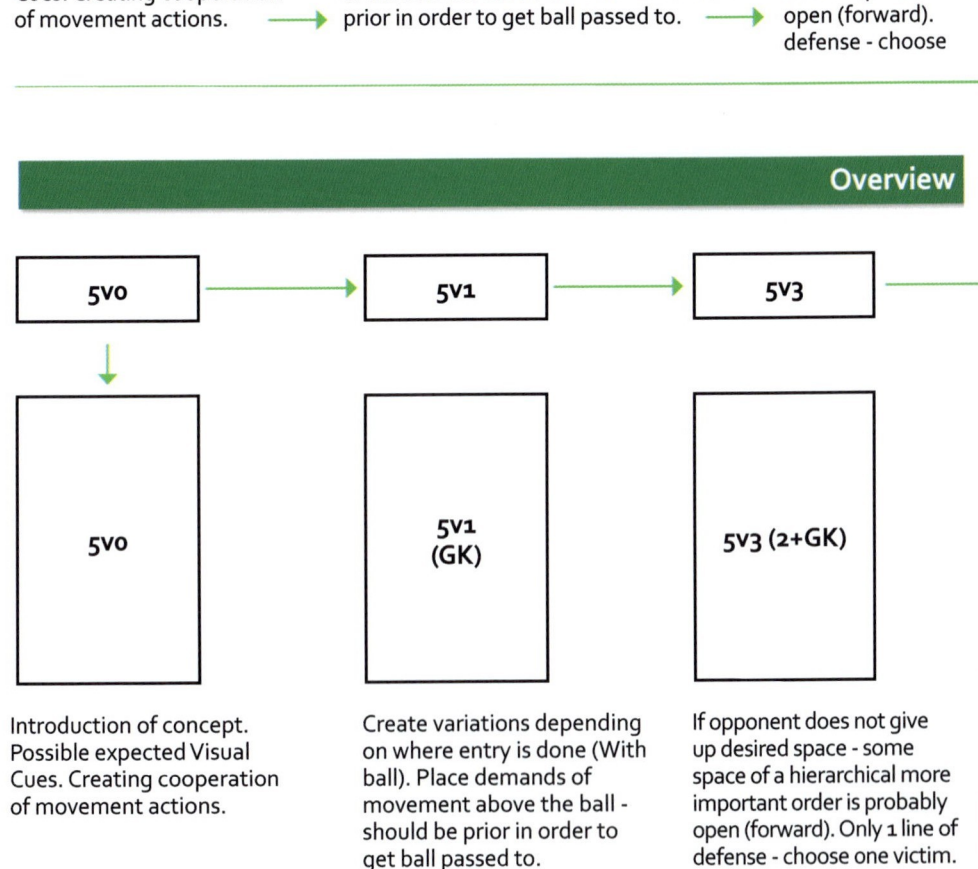

| 5v0 | 5v1(GK) | 5v3 (2+GK) |

Introduction of concept. Possible expected Visual Cues. Creating cooperation of movement actions. → Create variations depending on where entry is done (With ball). Place demands of movement above the ball - should be prior in order to get ball passed to. → If opponent does space - some space more important open (forward). defense - choose

Overview

| 5v0 | 5v1 | 5v3 |

| 5v0 | 5v1 (GK) | 5v3 (2+GK) |

Introduction of concept. Possible expected Visual Cues. Creating cooperation of movement actions.

Create variations depending on where entry is done (With ball). Place demands of movement above the ball - should be prior in order to get ball passed to.

If opponent does not give up desired space - some space of a hierarchical more important order is probably open (forward). Only 1 line of defense - choose one victim.

Figure 5.1

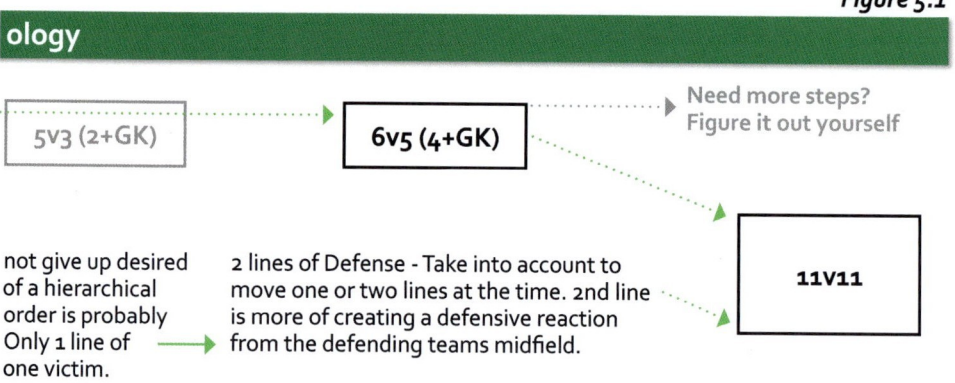

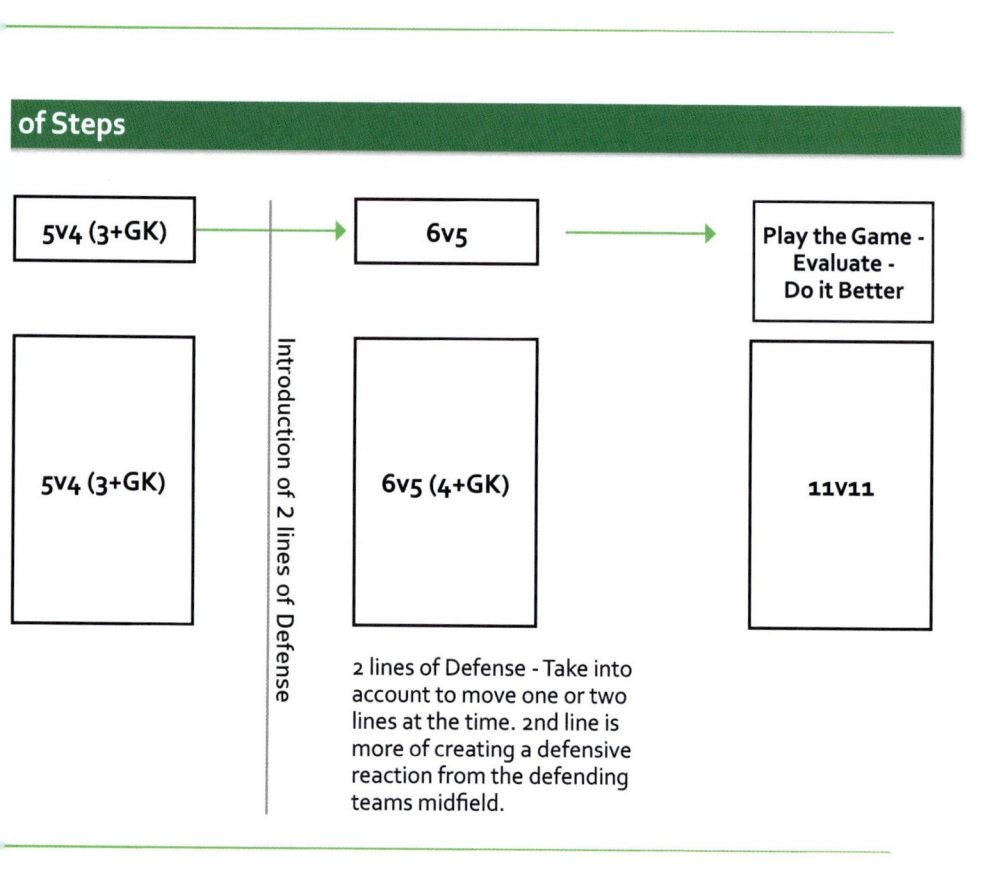

ology

5v3 (2+GK) ······▶ 6v5 (4+GK) ┄┄┄▶ Need more steps? Figure it out yourself

↘ 11V11

not give up desired of a hierarchical order is probably Only 1 line of one victim. ⟶ 2 lines of Defense - Take into account to move one or two lines at the time. 2nd line is more of creating a defensive reaction from the defending teams midfield.

of Steps

5v4 (3+GK)	⟶	6v5	⟶	Play the Game - Evaluate - Do it Better
5v4 (3+GK)		6v5 (4+GK)		11V11

Introduction of 2 lines of Defense

2 lines of Defense - Take into account to move one or two lines at the time. 2nd line is more of creating a defensive reaction from the defending teams midfield.

"PANIC"

What: 5v1 (5 offensive players vs 1 GK)
Why: Introduction to Interchanges in the lfinal third
How: Set up as suggested on the first picture. Outline space with cones or tape.

Coaching Points:
- Position - Moment - Direction - Speed*
- Make certain visual triggers are clear for the players (coach looks up to the 9 or 10 for example)
- Emphasize the angle of the passes, make it as game realistic as possible
- Put demands on the execution
- Create a competitive environment, for example players have to finish 3 out of 5 and so on
- Better to make 5 great than 25 bad - it's about quality - not quantity
- Don't wait on adding opponents - it creates more of a realistic scenario
- Look at the player runs - are there angles that they can adjust to improve the next situation?

Recommendations:
- As soon as possible, add opponents. Don't linger in 5v1 too long.
- Make your own cues, based on the context of the game and your players + opponents.
- 5v1 is a starting point
- You can be even more specific in your instructions to certain players - depending on your playing style
- Add another dimension - after finishing - make a defensive transition!
- Set demands! Football is played at 100% - but the learning process is crucial. Gradually increase demand for execution

Verheijen, R Periodisation in Football p. 42 World Football Academy

Starting positions for application of Interchanges

Objective:

To bypass an established backline in the last third of the pitch.

Description:

Players above the ball initiates the exercise.
The Coach passes the ball sideways.

Positional changes between 7-9-10-11. The player on the ball switches side and starts to the left.

Instructions:

Player on the ball (X) chooses which side is the best. For starters it might be a suggestion to start with the highest positioned player (9)

Thereafter we suggest to play

Players constantly change their starting positions.

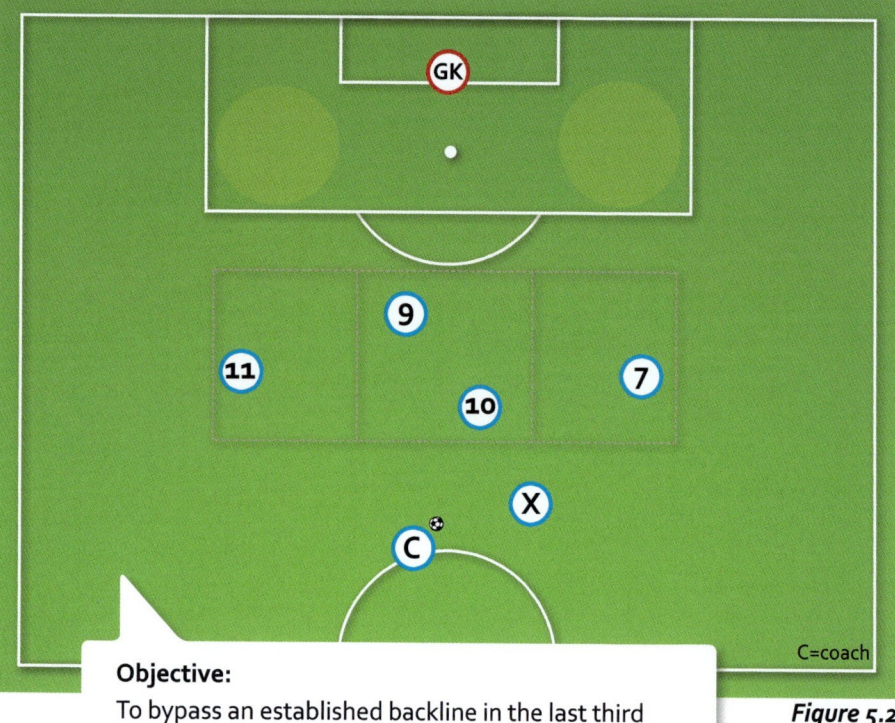

C=coach

Figure 5.2

"DEATH AT ONE'S ELBOW"

Interchange Exercise 1A

1. 9 and 11 switch positions
2. Coach passes the ball to the ballcarrier (typical midfield position)
3. Positional change between 11-7-10
4. The ballcarrier chooses the best passing option

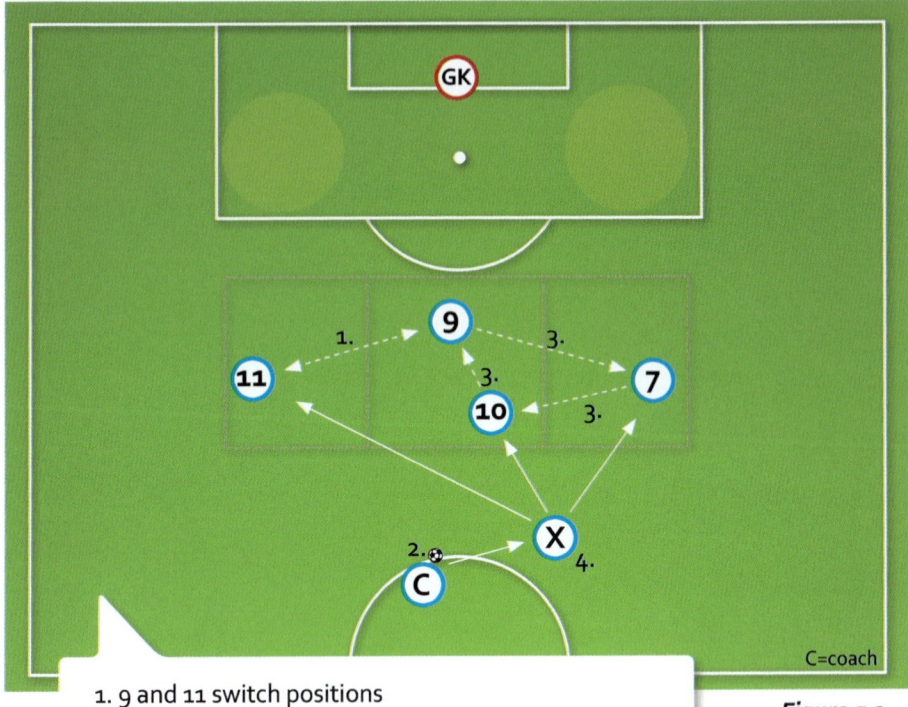

Figure 5.3

Interchange Exercise 1B

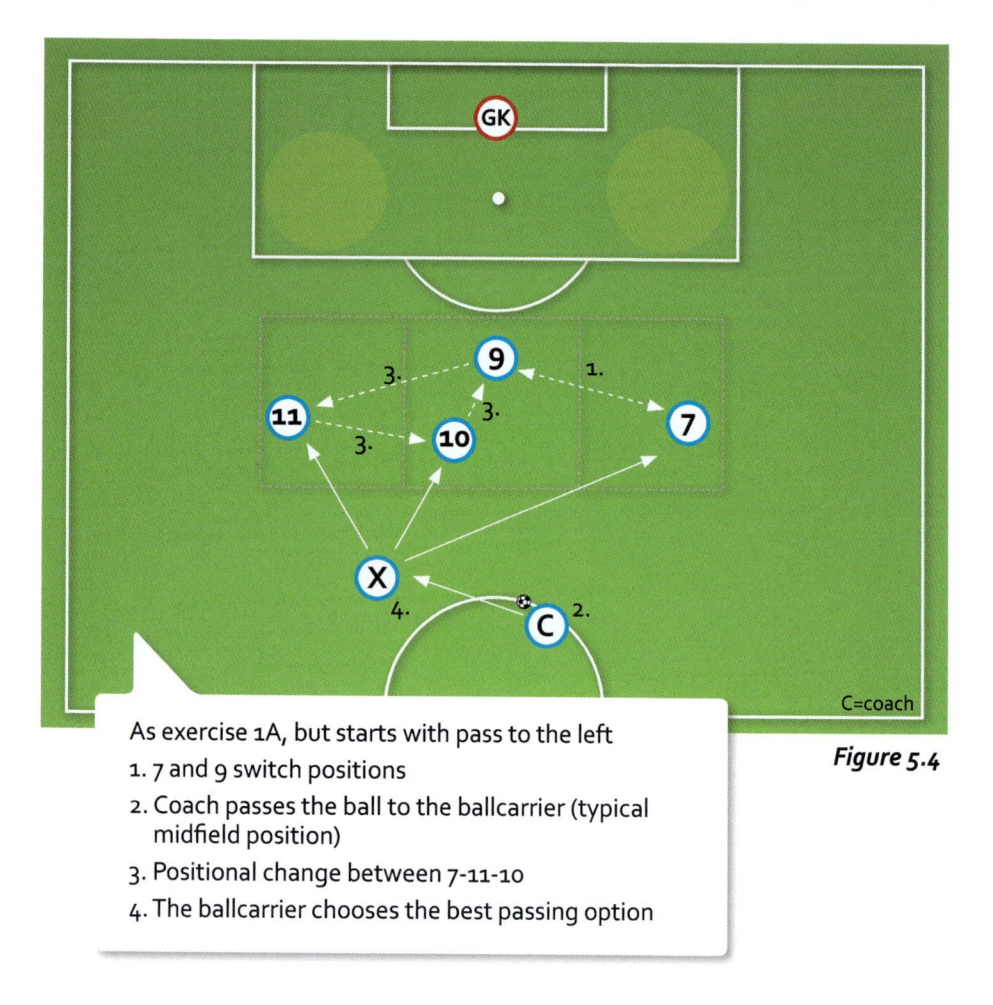

As exercise 1A, but starts with pass to the left
1. 7 and 9 switch positions
2. Coach passes the ball to the ballcarrier (typical midfield position)
3. Positional change between 7-11-10
4. The ballcarrier chooses the best passing option

Figure 5.4

"WELL I WONDER"

Interchange Exercise 2A

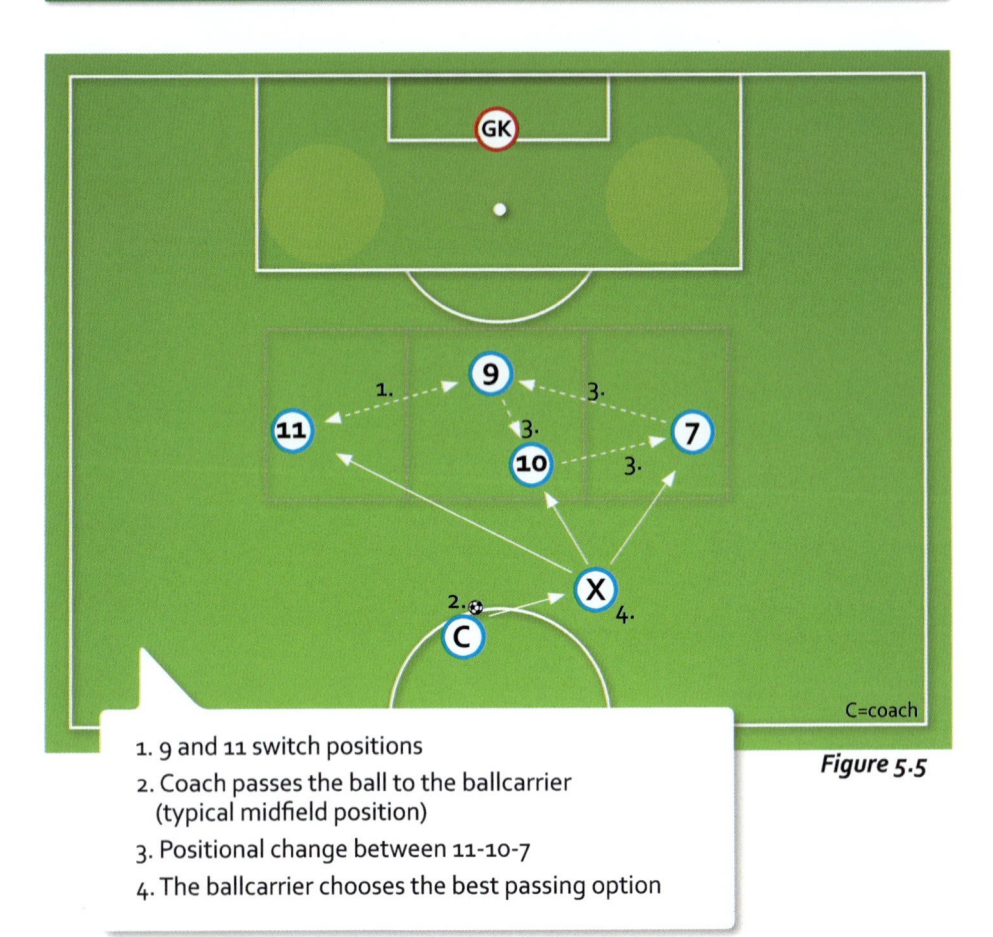

1. 9 and 11 switch positions
2. Coach passes the ball to the ballcarrier (typical midfield position)
3. Positional change between 11-10-7
4. The ballcarrier chooses the best passing option

Figure 5.5

Interchange Exercise 2B

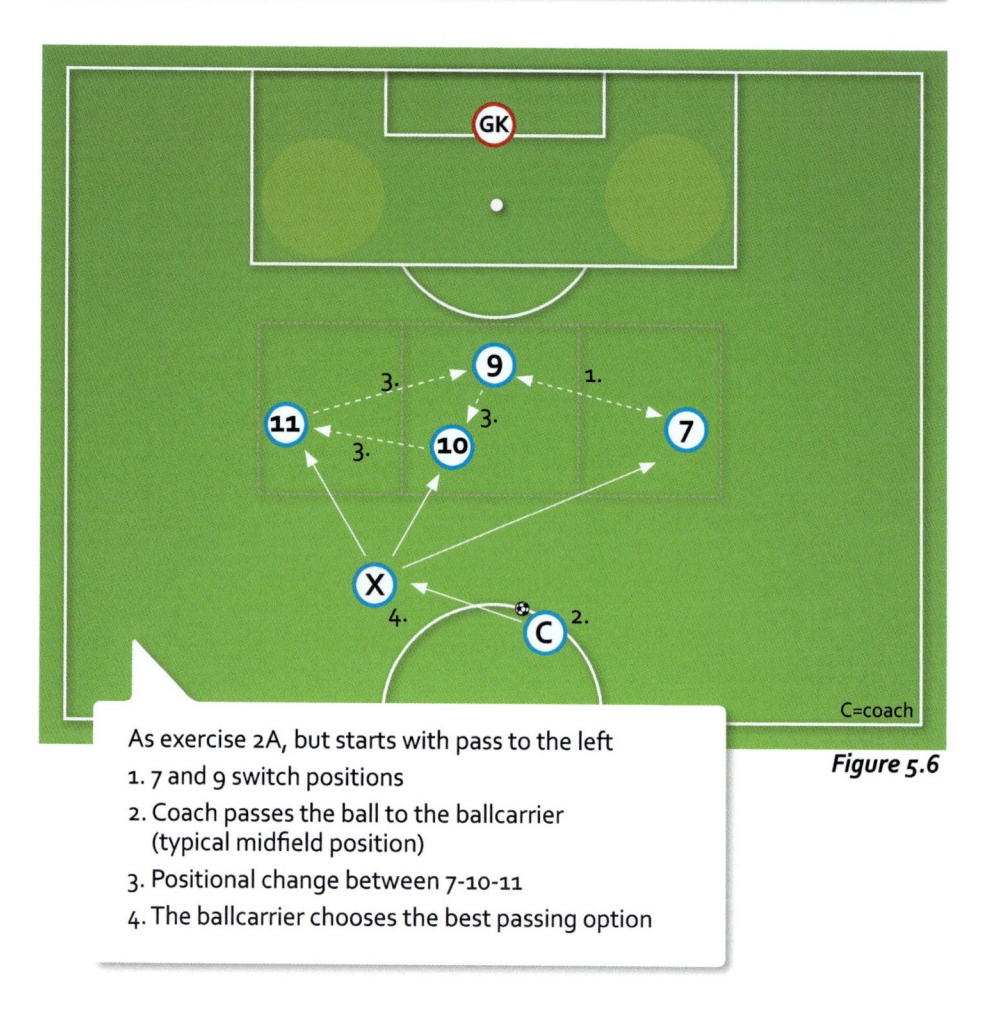

Figure 5.6

As exercise 2A, but starts with pass to the left
1. 7 and 9 switch positions
2. Coach passes the ball to the ballcarrier (typical midfield position)
3. Positional change between 7-10-11
4. The ballcarrier chooses the best passing option

"VICAR IN A TUTU"

Interchange Exercise 3A

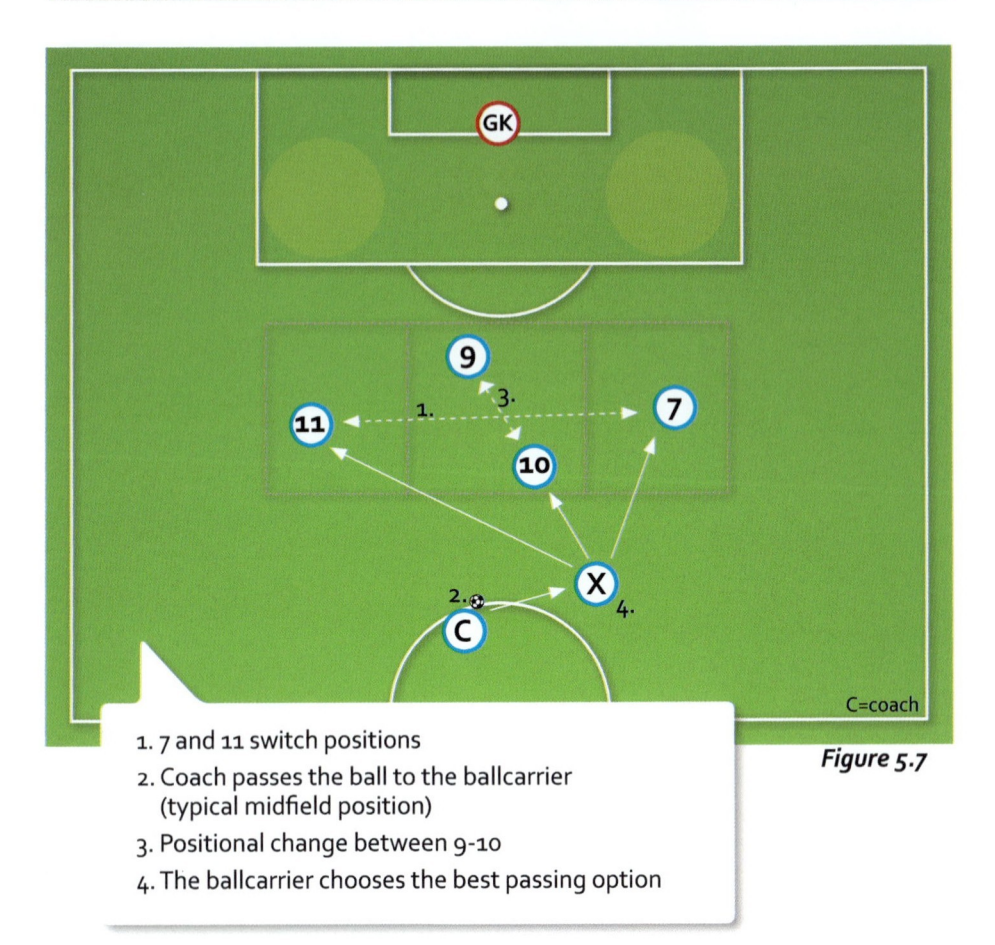

Figure 5.7

1. 7 and 11 switch positions
2. Coach passes the ball to the ballcarrier (typical midfield position)
3. Positional change between 9-10
4. The ballcarrier chooses the best passing option

C=coach

Interchange Exercise 3B

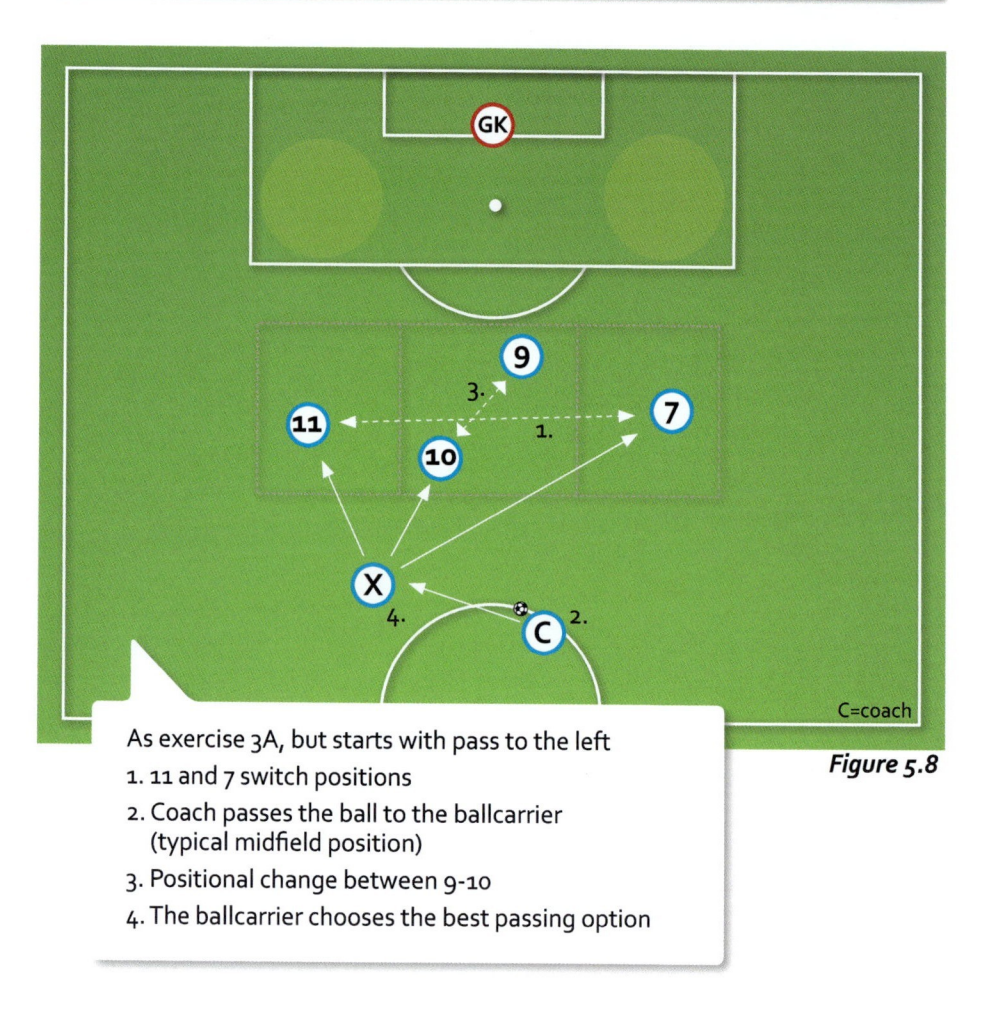

As exercise 3A, but starts with pass to the left
1. 11 and 7 switch positions
2. Coach passes the ball to the ballcarrier (typical midfield position)
3. Positional change between 9-10
4. The ballcarrier chooses the best passing option

Figure 5.8

C=coach

"THAT JOKE ISN'T FUNNY ANYMORE"

Interchange Exercise 4A

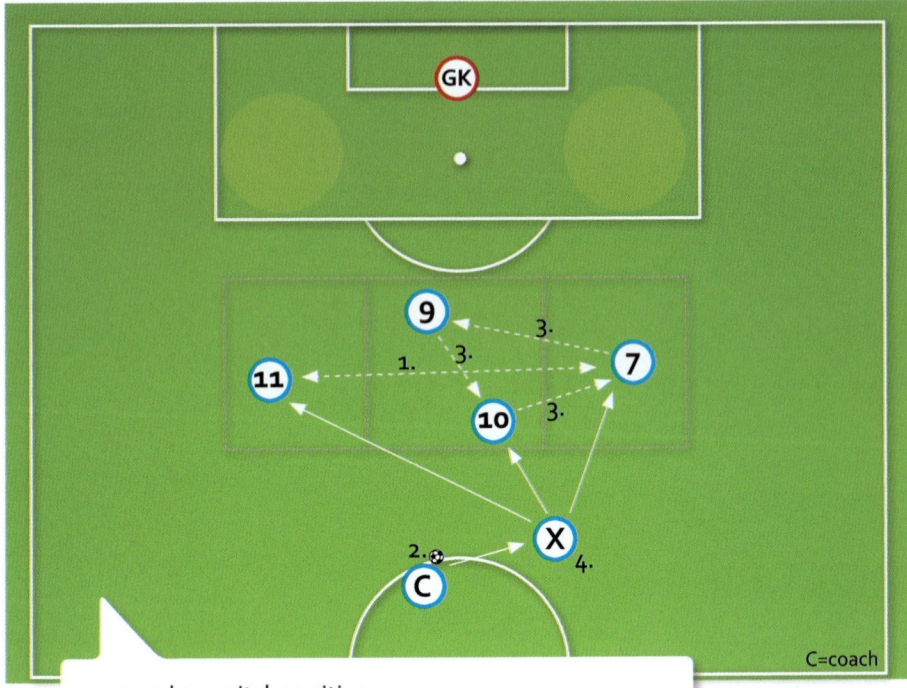

Figure 5.9

C=coach

1. 7 and 11 switch positions
2. Coach passes the ball to the ballcarrier (typical midfield position)
3. Positional change between 11-9-10
4. The ballcarrier chooses the best passing option

Interchange Exercise 4B

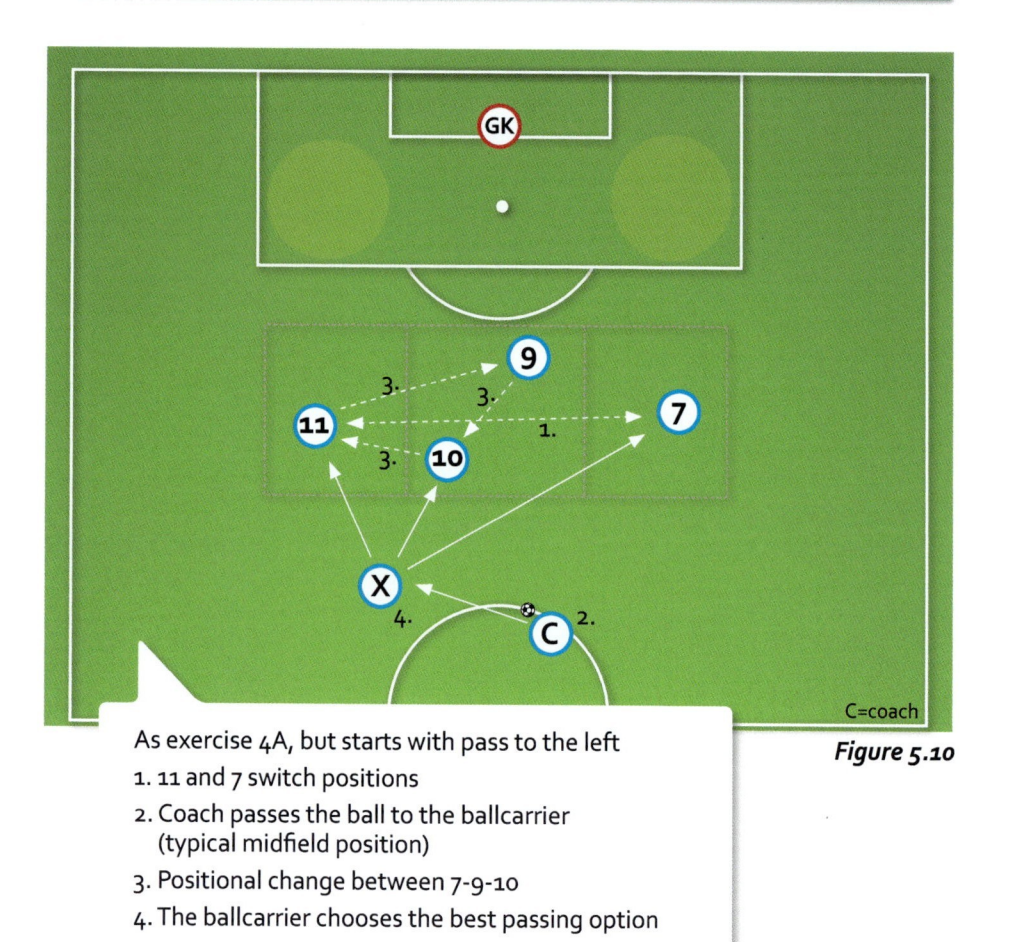

As exercise 4A, but starts with pass to the left
1. 11 and 7 switch positions
2. Coach passes the ball to the ballcarrier (typical midfield position)
3. Positional change between 7-9-10
4. The ballcarrier chooses the best passing option

Figure 5.10

"ASK"

Interchange Exercise 5A

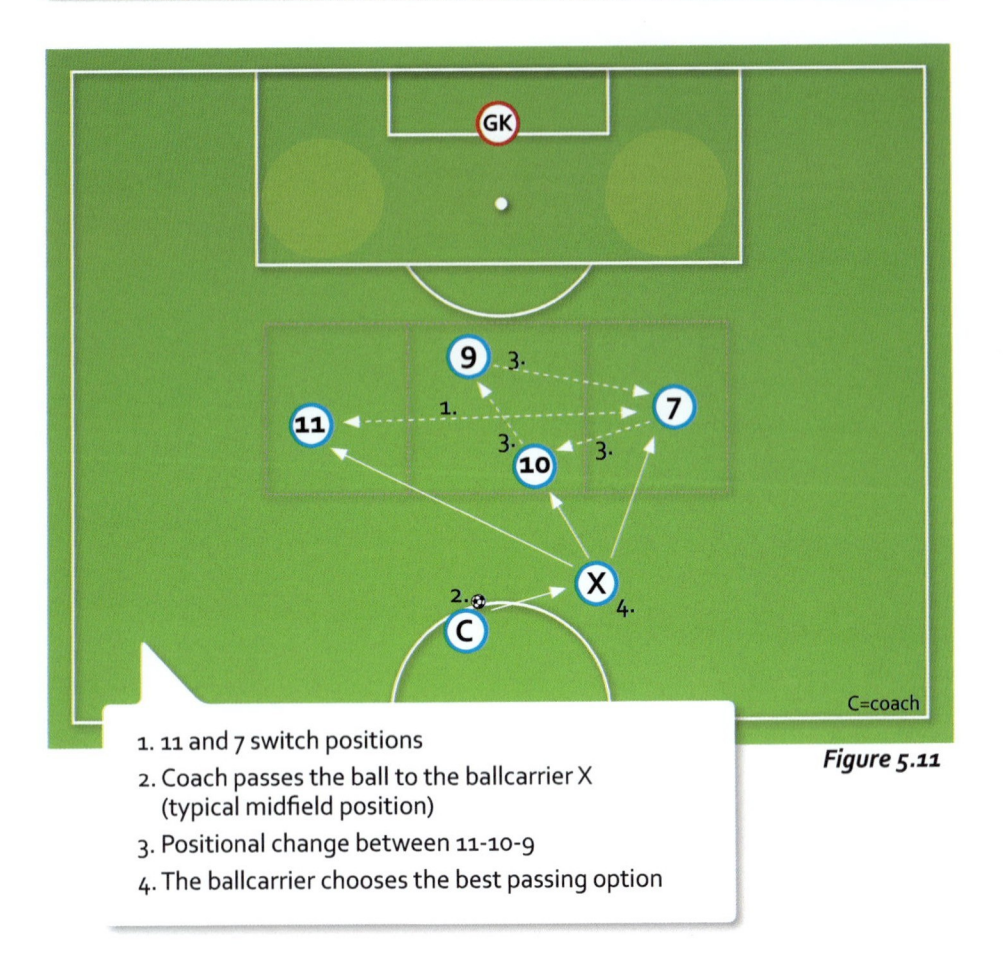

1. 11 and 7 switch positions
2. Coach passes the ball to the ballcarrier X (typical midfield position)
3. Positional change between 11-10-9
4. The ballcarrier chooses the best passing option

Figure 5.11

C=coach

Interchange Exercise 5B

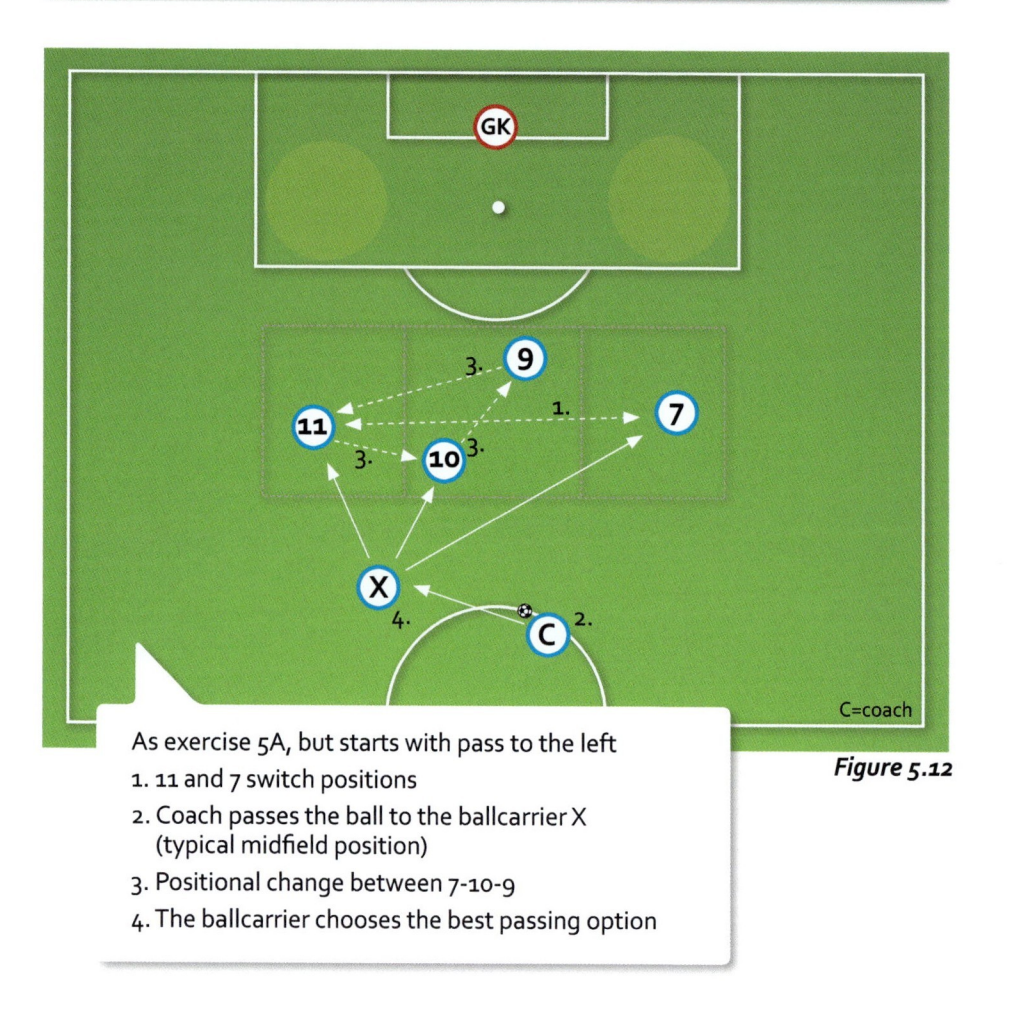

As exercise 5A, but starts with pass to the left
1. 11 and 7 switch positions
2. Coach passes the ball to the ballcarrier X (typical midfield position)
3. Positional change between 7-10-9
4. The ballcarrier chooses the best passing option

Figure 5.12

C=coach

"HAND IN GLOVE"

Interchange Exercise 6A

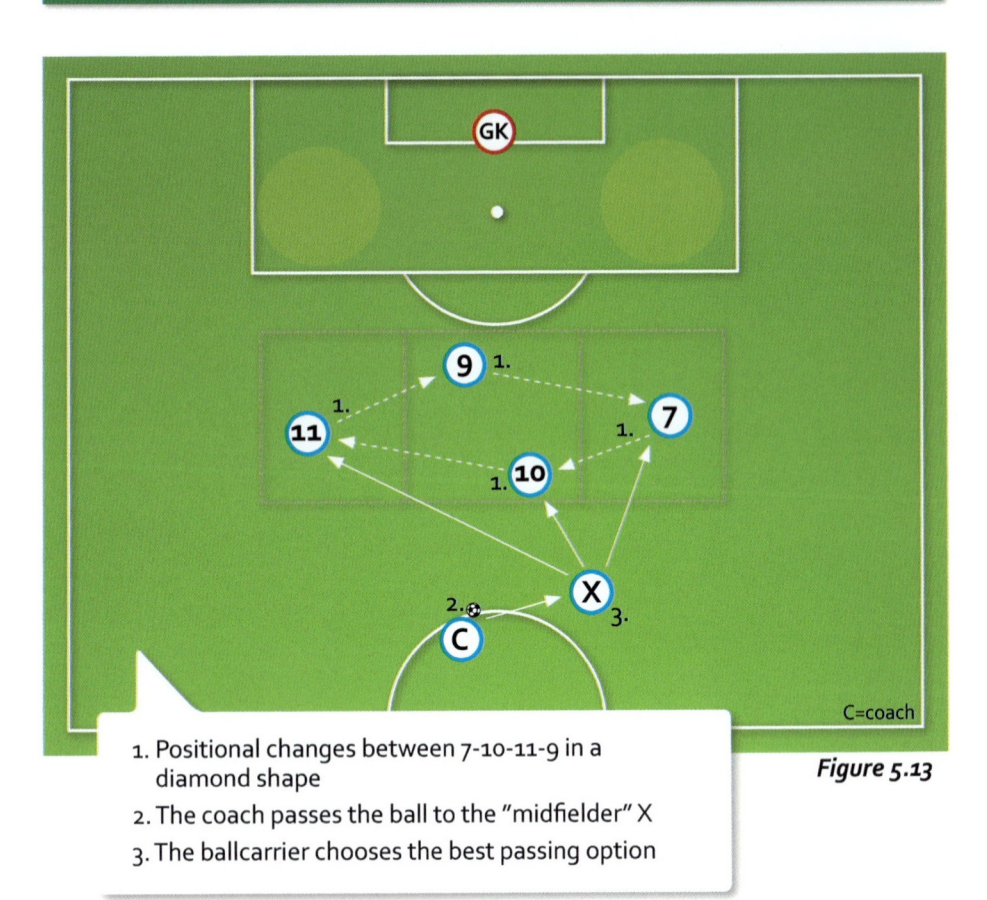

Figure 5.13

C=coach

1. Positional changes between 7-10-11-9 in a diamond shape
2. The coach passes the ball to the "midfielder" X
3. The ballcarrier chooses the best passing option

Interchange Exercise 6B

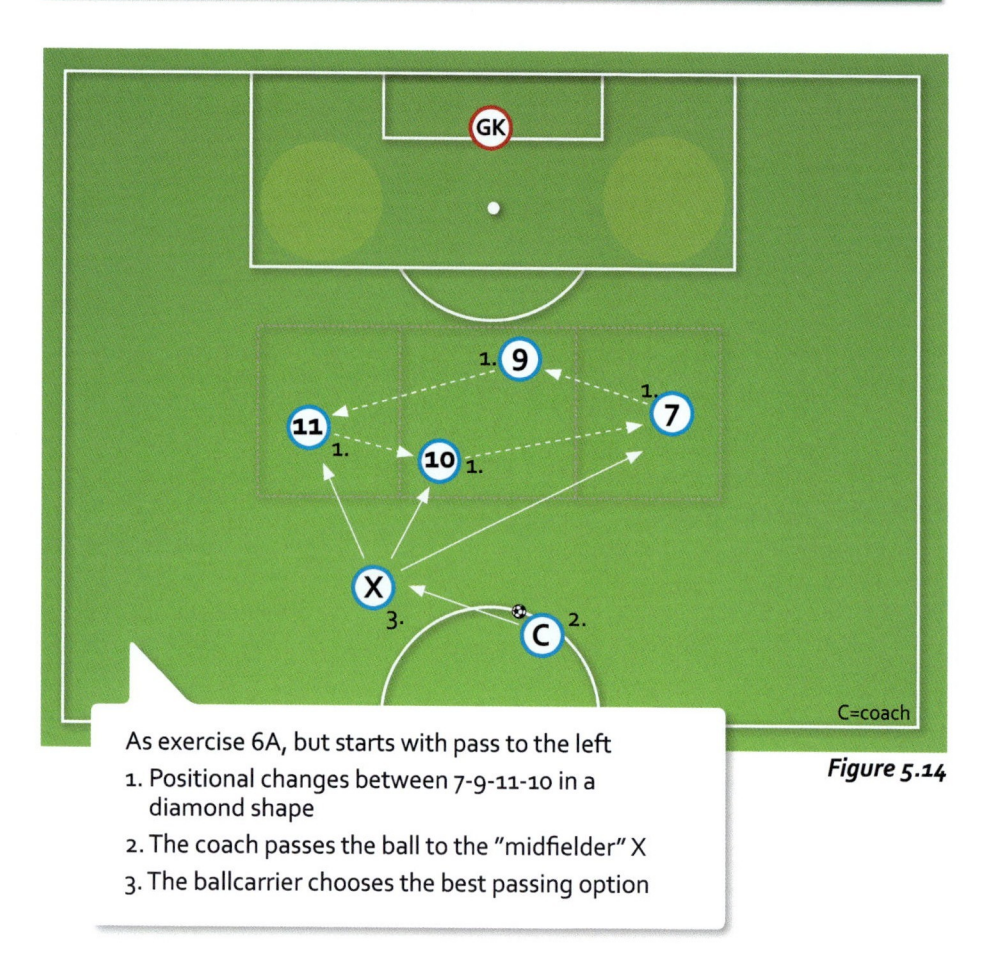

As exercise 6A, but starts with pass to the left
1. Positional changes between 7-9-11-10 in a diamond shape
2. The coach passes the ball to the "midfielder" X
3. The ballcarrier chooses the best passing option

Figure 5.14

C=coach

"ASLEEP"

Interchange Exercise 7A

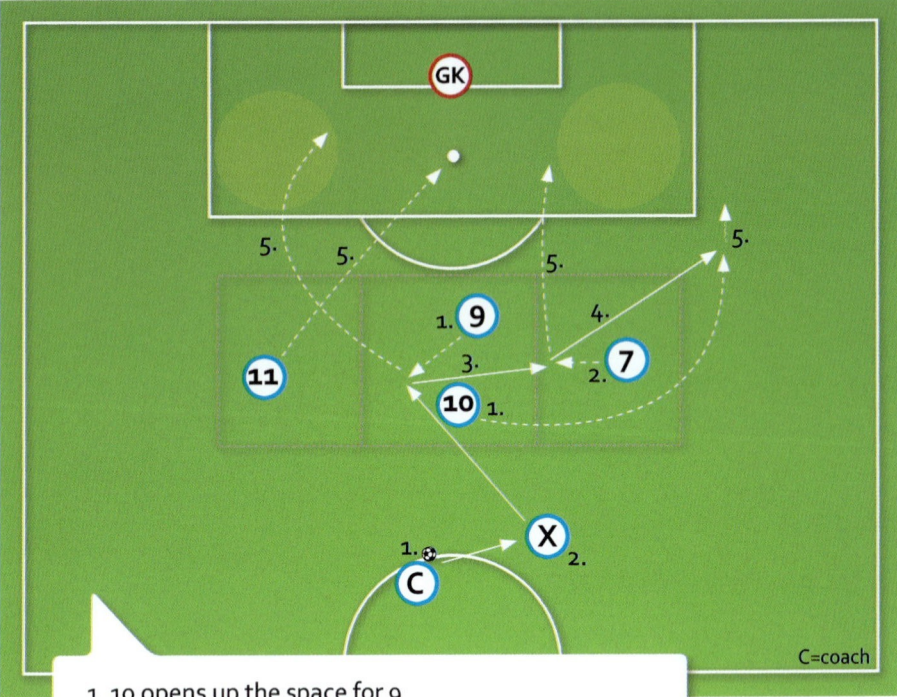

Figure 5.15

1. 10 opens up the space for 9
1. Coaches passes the ball sideways to the "midfielder"
2. 10 runs for an overlap for 7 who finds the "pocket"
3. 9 passes to 7
4. 7 turns with the ball facing the goal and plays 10
5. 10 drives the ball and looks for a cross/or to play the ball into the halfspace
5. 7-9-11 seeks positions for a shot at the goal
6. Defensive transition from 7-9-11-10 after the finish

C=coach

Off Goal 1

Interchange Exercise 7B

As exercise 7A, but starts with pass to the left
1. 10 opens up the space for 9
1. Coaches passes the ball sideways to the "midfielder"
2. 10 runs for an overlap for 11 who finds the "pocket"
3. 9 passes to 11
4. 11 turns with the ball facing the goal and plays 10
5. 10 drives the ball and looks for a cross/or to play the ball into the halfspace
5. 7-9-11 seeks positions for a shot at the goal
6. Defensive transition from 7-9-11-10 after the finish

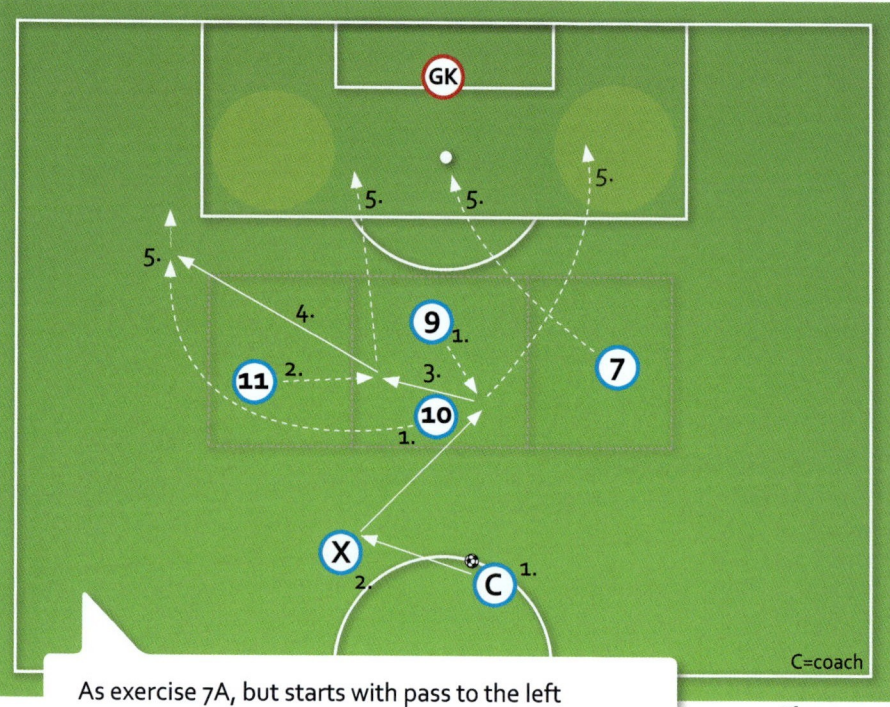

C=coach

Figure 5.16

"PLAY WITH FIRE"

Interchange Exercise 8A

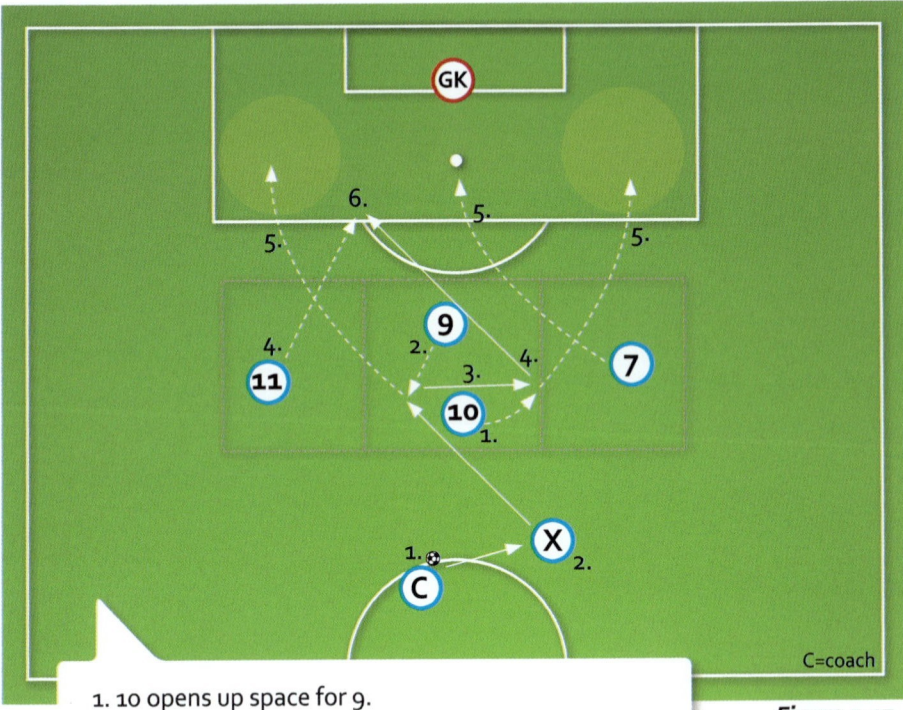

Figure 5.17

1. 10 opens up space for 9.
1. Coach passes the ball sideways to "midfielder" X
2. Ballcarrier seeks nr 9
3. 9 passes the ball to 10
4. 11 makes a deep run and 10 looks to pass the ball
5. 7-9-10 seeks positions for the finish
6. 11 goes for the shot or cross
7. Defensive Transition from 7-9-10-11 after finish

Interchange Exercise 8B

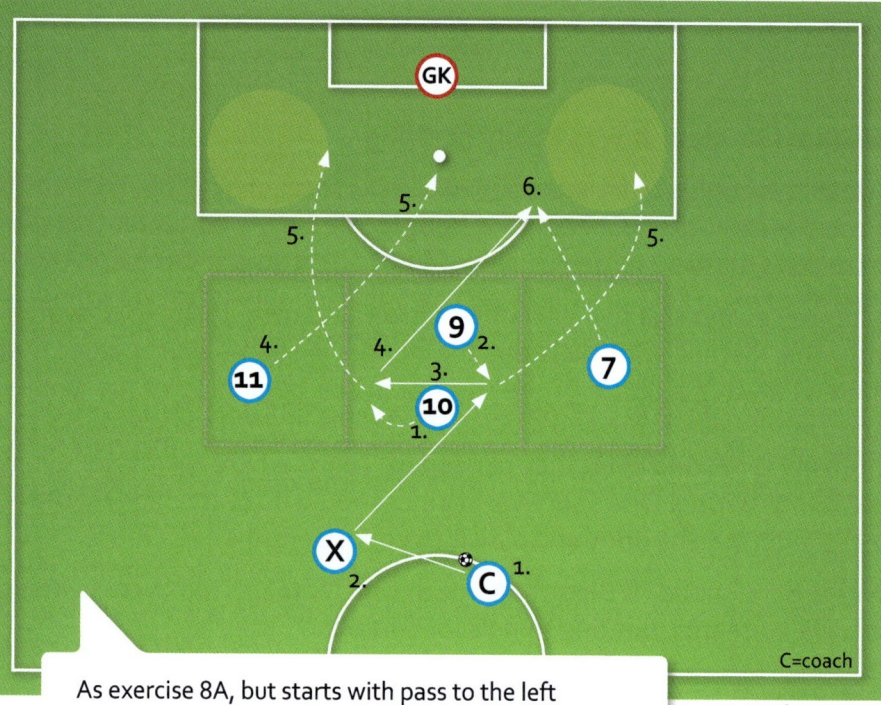

As exercise 8A, but starts with pass to the left
1. 10 opens up space for 9.
1. Coach passes the ball sideways to "midfielder" X
2. Ballcarrier seeks nr 9
3. 9 passes the ball to 10
4. 7 makes a deep run and 10 looks to pass the ball
5. 11-9-10 seeks positions for the finish
6. 7 goes for the shot or cross
7. Defensive Transition from 7-9-10-11 after finish

Figure 5.18

C=coach

WHITE RABBIT

Build Up

Where do you most probably score goals? Right, it's probably in front of you and in the opponent's penalty area. So therefore, all the priorities in a build up should be that the ball ends up there as frequently as possible. The means is not the goal itself, goals are.

There are very clear examples in the build up where the interaction between the different lines is on a different level.

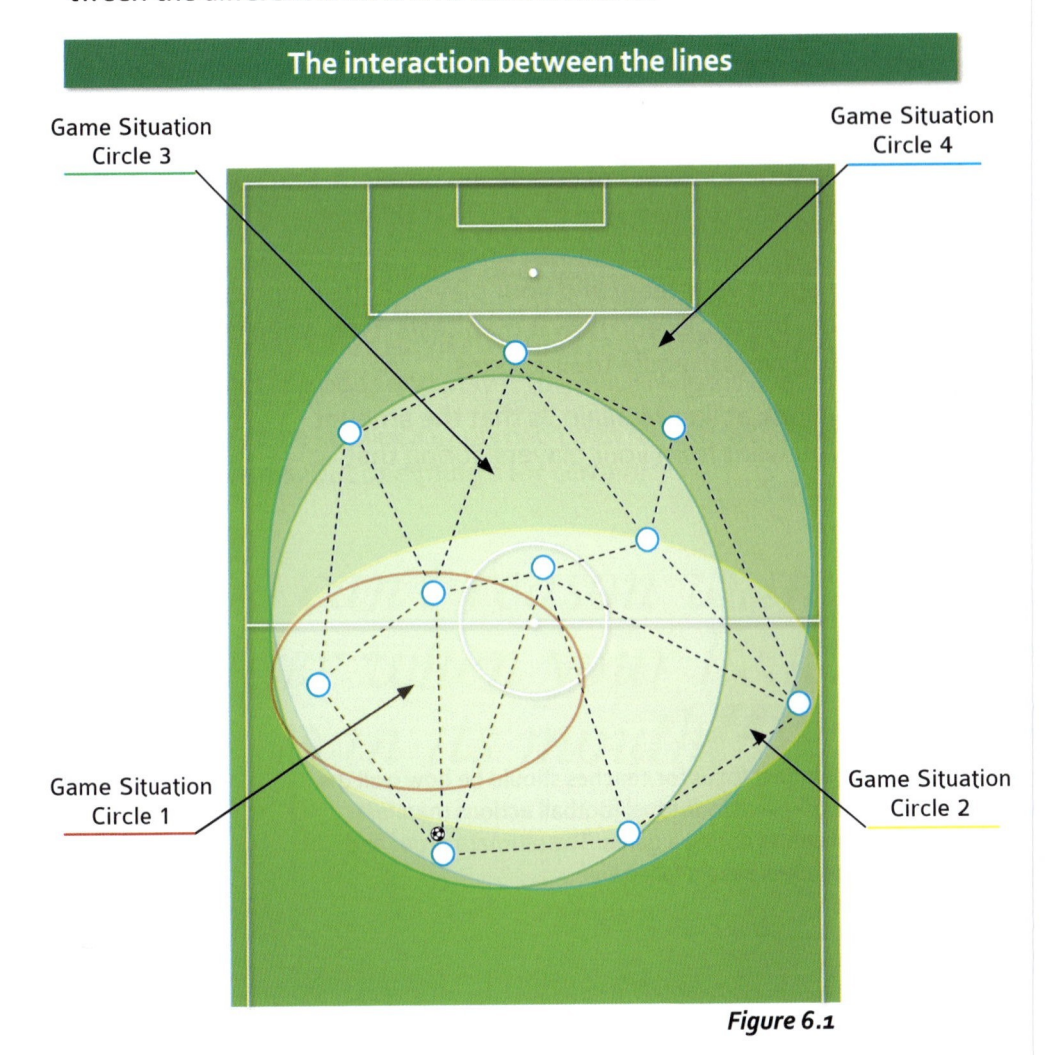

The interaction between the lines

Game Situation Circle 3

Game Situation Circle 4

Game Situation Circle 1

Game Situation Circle 2

Figure 6.1

An example of a classic interaction with a center back who has the ball - a striker pushes the backline higher up. And here's the thing - there's nothing wrong with just that. But - and there is actually a clear but. What I just described was an instance of communication (interaction) between two players. What if the demands were a bit different:

1) You would ask one of your central midfielders to open up a passing lane for the center back

2) One of your other central midfielders would give support to the striker

3) Furthermore - asking one of the wingers (left or right) to move inside between the opponents midfield and backline

4) Give instructions to the left back to push up into the left half space - to act as a second option for the center back to use if the striker is not available for the pass forward.

5) And one of the wingers (left in this case) pushes down the last line if the opposite gives support.

[7] https://spielverlagerung.com/2016/03/07/how-to-create-a-game-model/

Welcome to Marcelo Bielsa's World - and this happens frequently during his games. For further reading on how to create and look at your Game Model - and more specifically in this case - Attacking-> Build Up, look at the excellent article at spielverlagerung.com[7]

More crystal clear principles that are in play, if you look more specifically, certain positions of that Atletico Bilbao Team are:

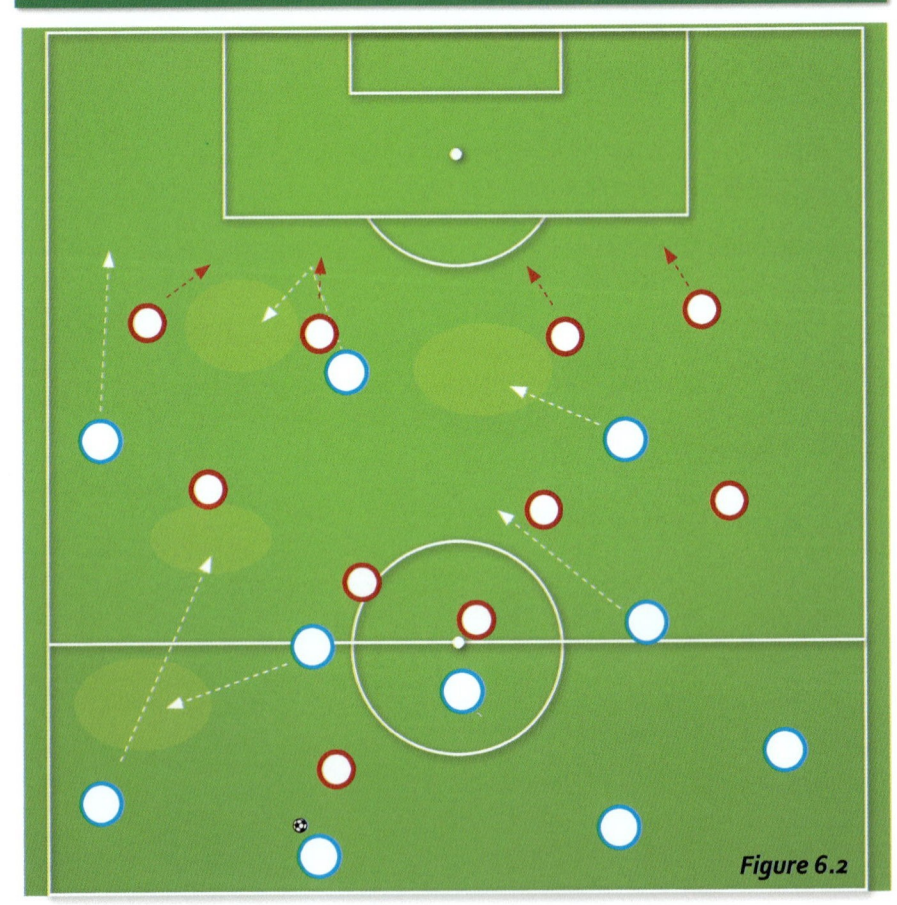

Interactions in build up

Figure 6.2

For further thinking:

Is there in Build Up anything you want to develop based on the characteristics of the players you have? Anything you want to improve, to make into a trademark?

Where are frequent game situations in a Build Up where your players might struggle in? How would you deal with these?

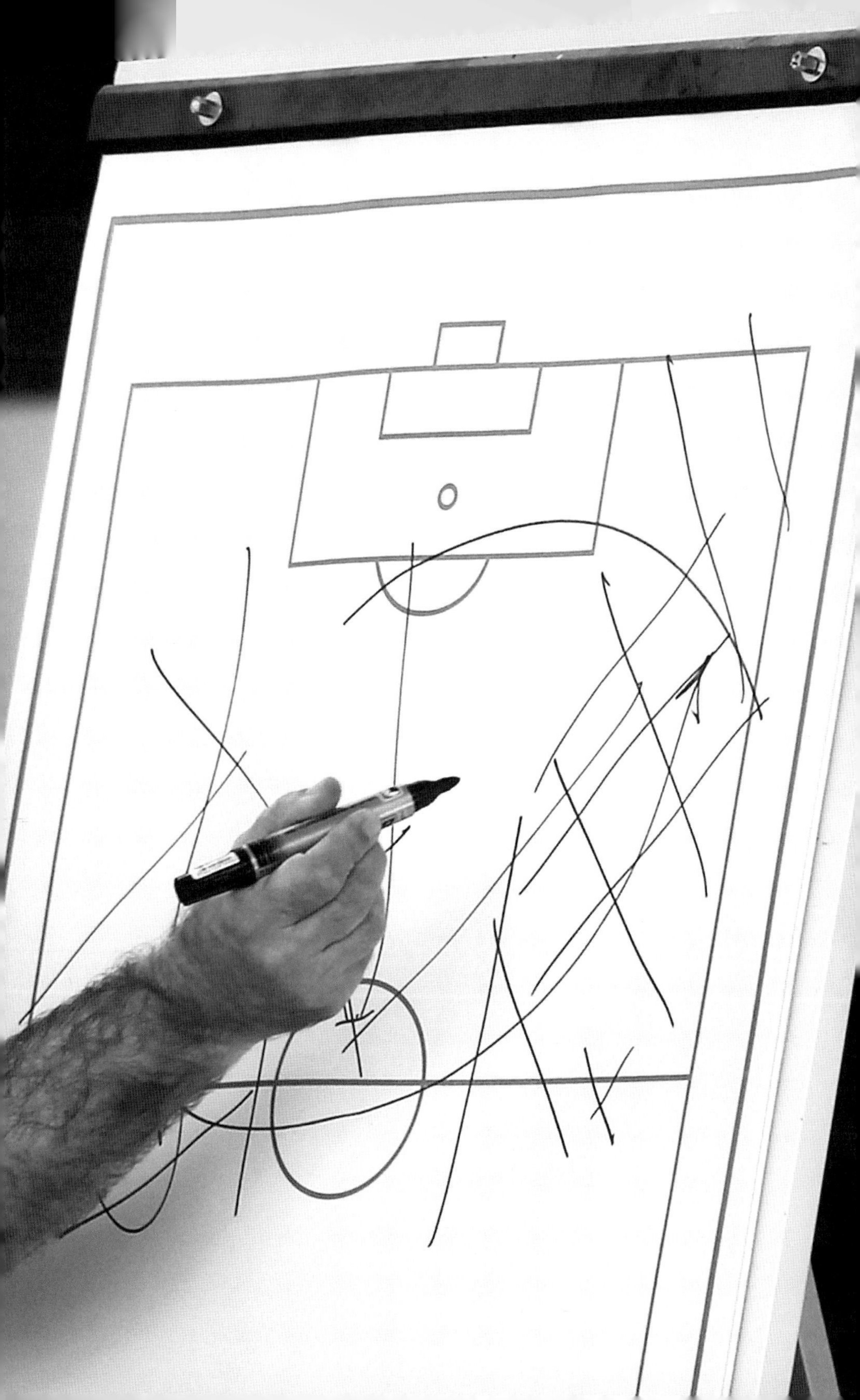

This is a hypothetical outline of how Atletico Bilbao built up and their principles in Attack against Manchester United.

	Attack - Build Up
Goalkeeper	- Bypass first line of opponent if possible - Be available for switch point of attack
Defenders	- Take space forward if possible - Bypass opponent through option 1) take space 2) bypass with a pass - Give support to midfielders - Be compact when attacking on the opponent's half
Midfielders	- Open up space so the ball can be played forward to the strikers - Rotate with other teammates both vertically and horizontally
Strikers	- Find attractive space in the current game situation - Push the opponents last line down - but don't work to close to the last line - Drag opponents out of position with movement actions - Hold up the last line in the attacking third

This is purely hypothetical principles on how Bilbao faced United. The game specific plan is owned by the involved players and staff.

Attack - Create Goal Scoring Chances

- Take a position further up the field

- If possible join the attack with runs into the box
- Uphold balance if needed to prevent possible transitions

- Create overloads by running past the opponents last line
- Create crossing situations
- Overload any corridor where the ball is situated (Numerical Overload)

- Runs into the Golden Zone (when a crossing situation arises)
- Position yourself for lay-offs for 3rd man
- Interchange positions with other strikers

Figure 6.3

ENTRIES

Please, Please, Please Let Me Get What I Want This Time
I can still remember. These two games, still create a shiver to our core. The tenacity the Bilbao players had, when they ran rampage both at Old Trafford and San Mamés. A core principle, is that no matter the situation - it needs to create a positive entry and bypasses the opponent, all according to Bielsasism. The following events reoccur:

- A deep run beyond the last line of defense
- Always try and reach an end product, encourages players to find solutions to move forward and not recede and play the ball backwards unless they really must
- Overloading the opponent in the vertical corridor in order to create open space elsewhere
- After one action performed, really quick to perform a new dynamic action or football action.
- In a controlled build up vs an organized opponent, always 4 or more players in the box

Outline of Entries.
We have added a couple of game situations for you - and to really get more of a grip of the attacking power and frequency Bilbao was showing against Man Utd. But there were still times when Bielsa was not quite satisfied about the performance, which speaks more about the standards he's asking for in his players than the actual performance from Bilbao. A new standard - an epic one too.

How to create a possible entry?

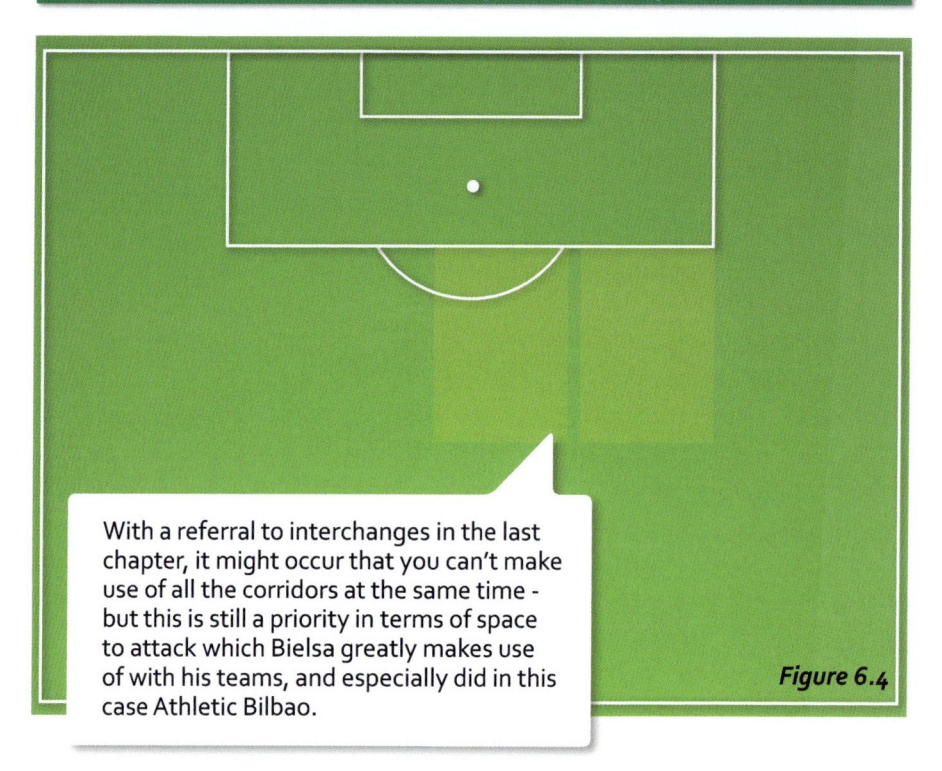

With a referral to interchanges in the last chapter, it might occur that you can't make use of all the corridors at the same time - but this is still a priority in terms of space to attack which Bielsa greatly makes use of with his teams, and especially did in this case Athletic Bilbao.

Figure 6.4

Bielsasism

A way to create a "positive entry" is to *make use of more players coming from lower position, in this case a 5th player joining and attacking the space in behind fullback in this case.

Entry Man U

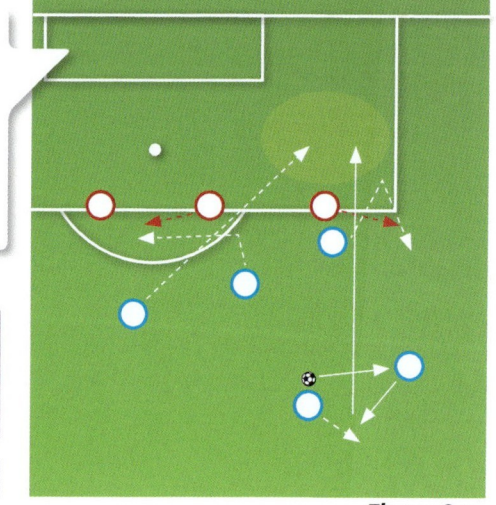

Figure 6.5

103

07 SUMMARY

This book has been divided into three obvious blocks:
1) **Objective Football Principles**
2) **Rotations**
3) **Interchanges**

What we've tried to do is to place the rotations and interchanges in as objective of frame as possible. With a great amount of respect for Marcelo Bielsa, we have been inspired by him through meticulous viewing of games, recorded training sessions, and the few interviews which are out there. And by positioning him as a "Madonna of Football", we've tried to preserve his mystique as much as possible. His work needs to serve as an inspiration to us all, an enigma.

To summarize rotation is the axis of creating space in a horizontal and vertical way, simultaneously on at team level.
This is about creating a reference for your team project, with a recognizable challenge to resolve.

The didactic questions, on a methodological level are a questions which still haunt me (John) today - I've tried to give as much insight on these as possible. How do I start and how should I continue to evolve and therefore develop the players I have at hand? And looking back, I've always tried to start with smaller numbers, instead of looking at the bigger picture (11v11) as the starting point. An exercise is never a starting point.

Interchanges is the term describing the change of positions between multiple players in order to create a goalscoring opportunity. The effect of a positional change is that it generates confusion for the opponents, and before they know what really happened - the ball has bypassed them.. We both are at times frustrated by stupidity in how teams try to attack their opponents, with little or no outcome with their intentions.

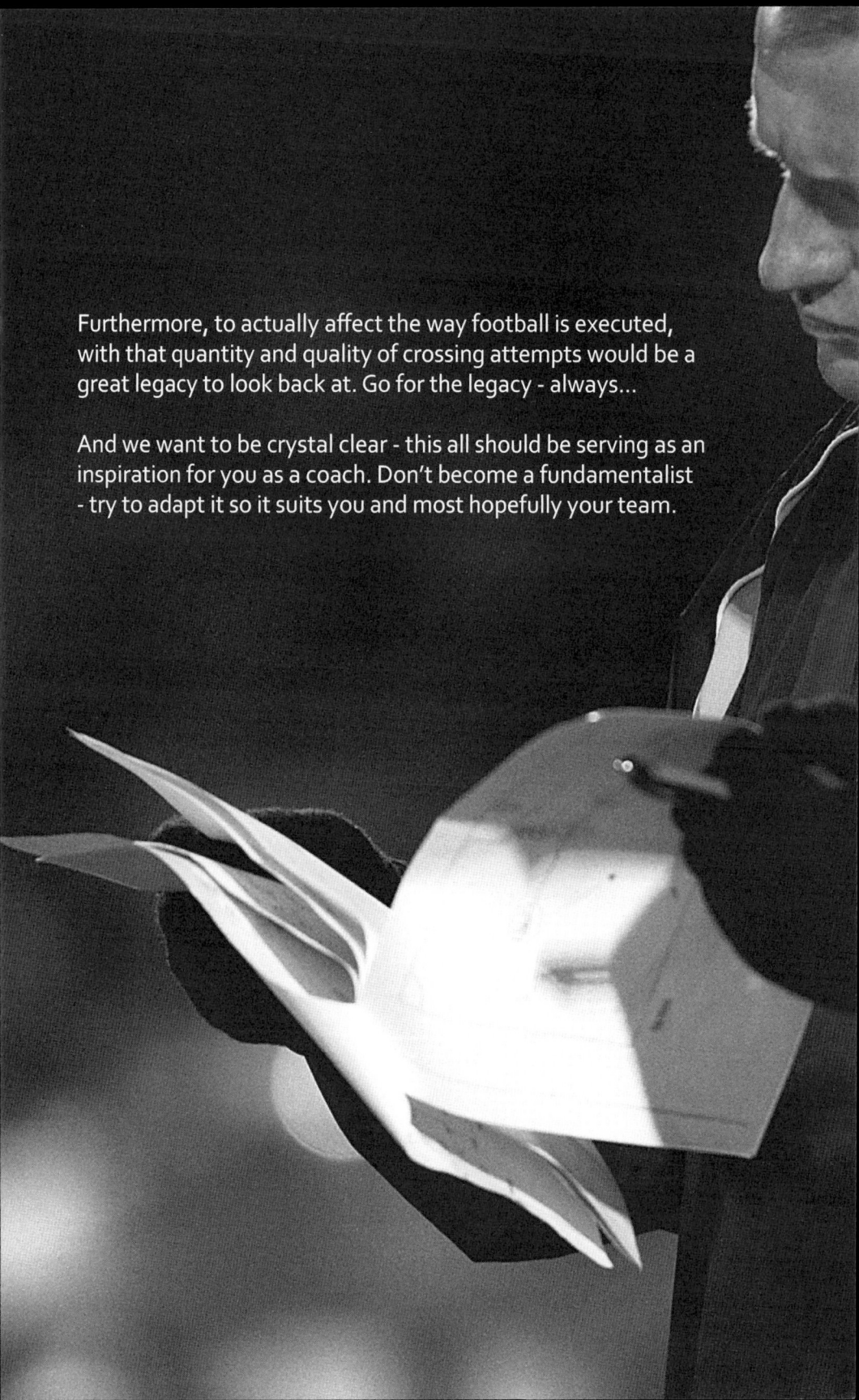

Furthermore, to actually affect the way football is executed, with that quantity and quality of crossing attempts would be a great legacy to look back at. Go for the legacy - always...

And we want to be crystal clear - this all should be serving as an inspiration for you as a coach. Don't become a fundamentalist - try to adapt it so it suits you and most hopefully your team.

THE PLATFORM

"Stretch out and Wait"

You've probably noticed the OCR links placed a little bit here and there. Although we feel that the book is something we made an effort with - we still want to keep you inside the rabbit hole. All videos are published for educational purposes only.

The Platform will be filled with content whereas the book can't really go because of physical limitations, so you'll find examples which we refer to in the book with video. Our sincere hope is that we will fill it with more content as we go - with articles - more videos and podcasts.

As a buyer of the book, we recommend you to visit our website **www.rotaciones.com**.

Use your smartphone to follow the QR code - use your camera and follow the link provided (should be the same for both Iphone and Android users).

All videos are for educational purposes only.

Platform

09 COACH EDUCATION

"Shoplifters of the World Unite"

Our aim of the education is to enlighten the way how a team can attack the opponent - and by doing so also take the decision making for the individual player to a higher level.

But the way to the players goes through the coaches - there is simply no other way. And we want to be there as potential educator for clubs - coaches - components of coaching courses - or as showcases.

Our clear aim is to make football in the world better - and the inspiration of Marcelo Bielsa has set us on a different path. How would you feel -if your team would be significantly improved at entries to create goalscoring chances, and at bypassing opposition lines with enhanced ease?

In all the theorizing about football, it's easy to forget that it is first and foremost a player's game. But having something that guides you when you're creating space - instead of just creating space for the sake of it - that's the actual thing that you want to bring out into the light. The potential joy it might bring, when the players know their ways - and can start to discover for themselves when and how to make use of this knowledge.

For further contact:
info@rotaciones.com

10 REFERENCES

"Heaven knows I'm miserable now"

Published

Verheijen, Raymond The original guide to Football Periodisation - Part 1 World Football Academy

Tamboer, Jan W.I, Lingen Bert, Verheijen Raymond Football Theory World Football Academy

Non printed sources

https://spielverlagerung.com/2016/03/07/how-to-create-a-game-model/ /Created by Maric, René

https://www.esdfanalysis.com/match-analysis/objectivity-subjectivity-philosophy-defending/ /Created by Josh Faga

https://www.ted.com/talks/tim_ferriss_why_you_should_define_your_fears_instead_of_your_goals

Finding Mastery 085 August 16, 2017 Shaka Smart: Bringing out the best in others. /Podcast with Michael Gervais

www.skolverket.se "Didaktik - vad, hur och varför" 2018-05-09 11.35

Sources of Inspiration

Morrissey, Johnny Marr, Andy Rourke, Mike Joyce

Marcelo Bielsa

Photos

Getty Images, Getty Images Sport